Compendium for Journal of Multi Business Model Innovation and Technology

Published, sold and distributed by:
River Publishers
Niels Jernes Vej 10
9220 Aalborg Ø
Denmark

River Publishers
Lange Geer 44
2611 PWDelft
The Netherlands
Tel.: +45369953197
www.riverpublishers.com

ISBN: 978-87-93379-41-1

Contents

The Business Model Cube

Peter Lindgren and Ole Horn Rasmussen

Department of Mechanical and Manufacturing Engineering, Aalborg University, Denmark

Received 10 September 2013; Accepted 25 September 2013

Abstract

The amount of literature concerning business model (BM) has increased in recent years (Zott 2010, Teece 2010, Krcmar 2011). A definition and a generic language of the BM have been long under way. Many of the existing BM frameworks are not empirically tested but are just BM concepts, which lead to a large variety of definitions in scholarly and practical literature.

A commonly accepted and generic language of the BM is therefore highly needed to embrace the opportunities but also challenges of business models and business model innovation (BMI). A commonly accepted BM language will enable the BM research to take one step further to become an accepted academic theory.

The paper attempts to fill in a piece of this gap in BM literature by proposing an empirically tested framework and language of BM by answering the research question:

- "What are the dimensions of any business model?"

This paper proposes that any business model has seven generic dimensions. The purpose of this paper is to verify and describe these dimensions. Previous BM concepts and related academic frameworks are compared to these seven dimensions.

A BM Cube is finally proposed as a generic framework for working with any business model. The BM Cube presents a new approach and framework to BM literature. Two case studies are used to show how the BM language and the BM Cube can be used in practice. The case study empirically documents the existence of the seven dimensions and that the BM Cube is useable when mapping "TO BE" and "AS IS" BM´s.

Keywords: Business model Cube, Business, Business model, Business and Business Model language, Business Model levels.

1. Introduction to the Business Model cube?

The first discussion on BMs can be traced back to an academic article in 1957 (Fielt, 2011). However, the concept did not gain acceptance until the mid-1990's (Fielt, 2011). The question — What is a BM? — has been raised, discussed and answered by many researchers in the last decade (Fielt, 2011). Porter (2001) argued that a "definition of a BM is murky at best. Most often, it seems to refer to a loose conception of how a business does business and generates revenue...." p. 73 (Porter, 2001). Morris *et al.* (Morris 2003), after reviewing existing theory on business models during late-1990's to 2003, concluded that a business's potential creation of value cannot be explained from the BM model theory, and that "a general accepted definition has not yet emerged" p. 8 (Fielt, 2011). However, Osterwalder *et al.* (2004) summed up academic work on BMs from the past 20 years, and stated that a definition of a BM broadly relates to a blueprint of how a business should conduct its business (Osterwalder, Pigneur, & Tucci, 2005). They further argue that a BM is a set of elements, which can be referred to as building blocks that, by their interrelation, express the logic of how a business earns money (Osterwalder, Pigneur, & Tucci, 2005).

Many academia have, in the past, been highly recognized for their approach to the BM concept (Fielt, 2011). Important to note is the distinction between business (Abell 1980) and BMs, as a business is in our framework considered to have one or more BMs i.e. the multi business model approach (Lindgren 2012). Furthermore, all BMs can be referred to either "AS IS" BM — already operating in the market or "TO BE" BM — being innovated or prepared to be introduced into the market (Lindgren 2012).

From the BM concept's infancy until today, it can be documented that the BM concept has naturally evolved and changed in relation to the BM context. Globalization and internet has increased businesses' interdependency and today businesses are connected in physical, digital and virtual networks (Choi 2003) (Daft, 2010) (Peng, 2010). Thereby, it is possible to utilize competences across businesses BM´s and BMs' boundaries in order to strengthen the BMI (Daft, 2010) (Lindgren 2012) of businesses. This tendency can be argued to have influenced the BM literature e.g. Chesbrough (2007) suggests that BMs should be opened i.e. Open Business Model (OBM), which includes that businesses should utilize the dimensions and components of BMs of other businesses within their BMs.

It has been argued that until 2007, the BM literature was primarily regarding closed BMs (CBMs), whereas BMs were bound to the focal business, and thereby not open to other businesses (Lindgren, 2011). The CBM argued by Chesbrough (2007) was not deemed fit in the global business model ecosystem, which requires openness and interfaces being able to comprehend interfacing with other businesses' BMs. Chesbrough (2007) further claims that CBMs delimit the potential value and effective use of BMI. BMI, as mentioned in the introduction, refers to the reinvention of current BMs dimensions or creation of new dimensions in order to create advantages to the business. Thus, Chesbrough's (2007) way of thinking of BMIs, as being open, has become the foundation of the development of a new and open network-based BM innovation concept. (Chesbrough, 2007) (Daft, 2010) (Lindgren, 2011). BMs are becoming more dynamic in their construction and today's BMs may easily be outdated for use tomorrow. Lindgren (2011) suggests that new BMs should serve as platforms for long-term and continuous BMI — and development of other BMs. Any business model is proposed as a platform for other BMs and BMI — thereby developing a multitude of BMs.

2. Introduction to the Business Model CUBE

Today, the term 'business model' is everyday and everybody´s language in business, and of business model academia´s. Even national governments, EU commission and US government use the term Business Model. The increased awareness of BMs (Zott 2010, Teece 2010, Casadesus-Masanell 2010, Krcmar 2011) have intensified the search for a generic business model language. However, with increased use and research of BM the fuzziness on how the BM really is constructed has increased even more.

The focus on being first with a generic and commonly accepted BM language has increased drastically in recent years (Taran 2009, Zott 2010, Fielt, 2011). The emphasis on the BM´s dimensions has been the topic of many academic papers and work (Magretta 2002, Osterwalder 2002, Johnson 2008, Chesbrough 2010, Osterwalder 2011, Krcmar 2011). Many have been focusing on the question of how many dimensions does the BM really consist of. Some propose 4, while others propose 6, 9 and 12 dimensions. This raises the question to, how is a business model really constructed and will we ever be able to find the generic dimensions and construction of the BM? Further, can we distinguish one BM´s construction from another BM or are they really built around the same generic dimensions?

These questions imply the increasing importance of thoroughly knowing and finding the dimensions of the BM. This question is also related to the question of when can we talk about a new BM — an incremental and/or radical changes of a BM (Peng, 2010)(Lindgren, 2011) and does that influence the generic construction of the BM.

The focus in this paper is therefore primarily on the dimensions and construction of any BM although this is no longer deemed sufficient to cover the whole BM theory framework as it is just one focus of many — a fragmented part of the whole business model environment, research and discussion. Today, the focus of the BM seems to be changing towards a more holistic BM discussion taking in the BM´s relations to other BMs and the BM´s environment — leaving the basic BM dimensions and constructions behind. The focus of the OBM (Chesbrough, 2007) (Daft, 2010) and the innovation of BM (Osterwalder , 2011) seems to have taken nearly all research attention.

In an ever-changing and increasingly competitive global market, which according to Friedman (2007) is a result of the ongoing process of globalization and business model change, Chesbrough (2007) emphasizes the need for even more BMIs, including developing open and different businesses models. However, how can a business follow this advice without knowing the basic construction of the BM? As the basis of any BM discussion, we must begin by understanding, defining and testing the generic construction of the BM — in our sense what we call the dimensions of the BM.

In our study, we bridge BM frameworks from different business model frameworks to the BM CUBE concept (see Figure 1).

We try hereby to find BM dimensions that everybody seems to acknowledge and add those we believe are missing. We try to merge those dimensions, which are overlapping and we try to take out those dimensions that are not vital for a BM to operate. From this point of entry, we test our BM dimensions in two BM case studies to verify empirically our hypotheses of the existence of seven dimensions of any BM.

3. DESIGN/METHODOLOGY/APPROACH

The methodology applied in the paper is structured around deductive reasoning. First, a theoretical background of business model theory on each dimension of a BM is presented to provide a foundation for commonly accepted and acknowledged dimensions of a BM. To verify the existence of the dimensions of the BM and the usability of the BM cube, two business cases are presented — the Vlastuin Business Case and the HSJD business case. To “stress test” the generic use of the BM Cube framework, the cases represent two different businesses with different BMs. Both cases are also chosen to exemplify the

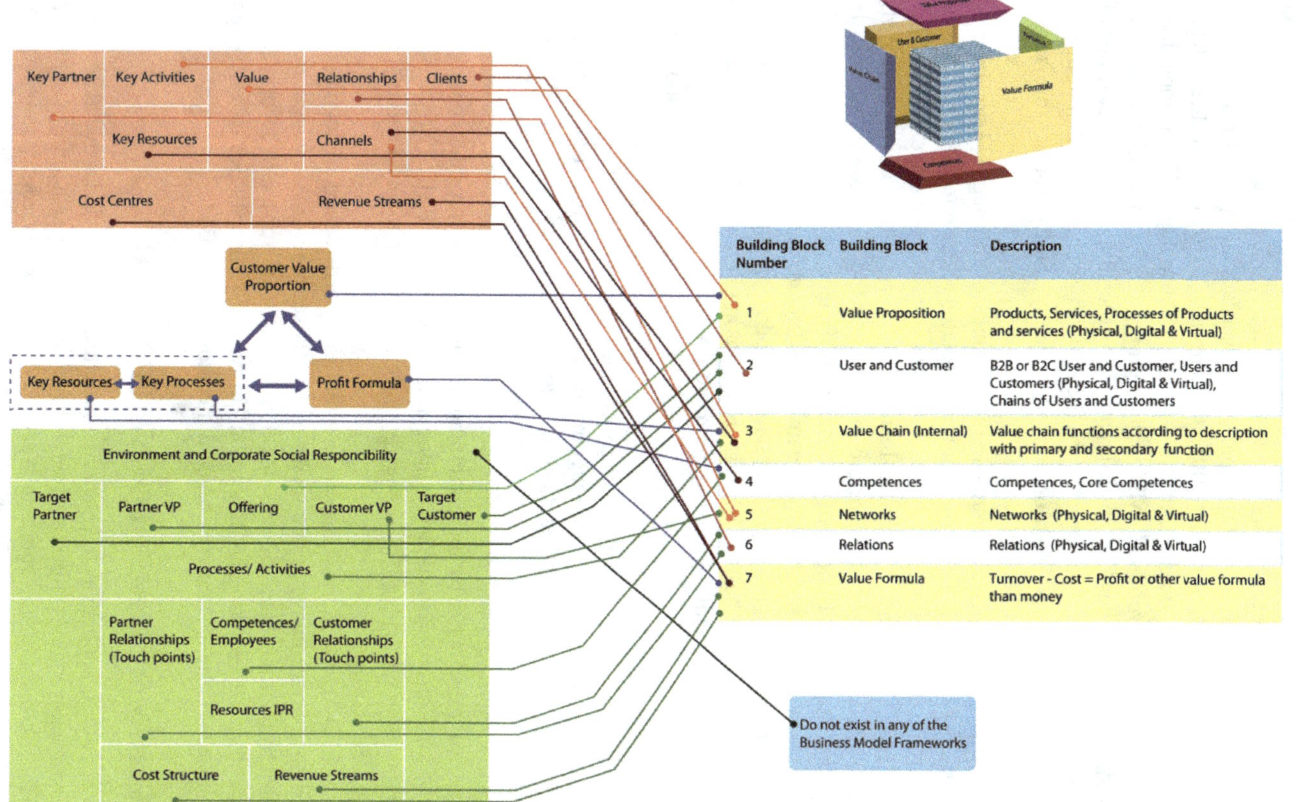

Figure 1 Illustration of comparison between different BM frameworks related to the BM Cube.

concept of the BM cube in use of "TO BE" and "AS IS" BM´s. "TO BE" BM´s are considered under construction — and maybe lacking one or more of the seven dimensions — and "AS IS" BMs are considered to be already operating in the market.

The information and data from the two cases are gathered through active participative research (Wadsworth 1998) carried out over three years in the EU FP 7 IOT project Neffics (NEffics 2013). Based on these cases supplemented with other empirical uses cases and tests, a final definition of the BM cube concept was formulated and is illustrated in the paper. A detailed test and confirmation of the BM cube is conducted and shown in the paper which has also been empirically tested in several other businesses (Appendix 0). The BM Cube has been tested in function with different use cases on the Neffics BM software platform (Neffics 2012) together with the Dutch ICT provider Cordys (www.Cordys.NL) and the Norwegian Software provider Induct (www.Induct.com). The BM Cube together with the VDML standard is being proposed in 2013 as an OMG standard (www.OMG.org).

4. DIMENSIONS, CONCEPTS AND LANGUAGE OF A BUSINESS MODEL

The term business has been defined by reputed academia from several dimensions. Abell (Abell 1980) defined a business by just three dimensions — **customer functions** — (values), **customer groups** (customers) and **customer technology** — (production technologies and process technologies). Porter (Porter 1985) argued that a business should be defined by its **suppliers, buyers** (customers) and **value chain activities**. (Hamel 1980) argued that a business could be defined by its **competences** and its **core competences.** Vervest (Vervest 2005) argued that a business could be defined by its **network** and how it organized its business together with network partners and Johnson (Johnson 2008) defined the business as how it created **value** to the **customer**. Håkonson (Håkonson 1980,Amidon 2008, Alee 2011, Russels 2011) defined the business from its **relations**. **Profit maximization** has been the central assumption in business and managerial economics (Henry and Haynes 1978) and the reasons for the stress on profits has been that it is the one pervasive objective running through all businesses; other objectives according to Henry and Haynes have been more a matter of personal taste or of social conditioning and were variable from business to business, society to society, and time to time. The survival of a business has until today very much been considered as depending upon its ability to earn profits where profits have been the business measure of its success (Henry 1978). The reason for profits emphasizing profits is also its convenience in analysis and it is easy to construct **formulae** on the assumption of profit maximization. It has been much more difficult to build models based on multiplicity of **value formulae**, especially when these formulae are concerned with nonmonetary factors as "fair", the improvement of public relations and e.g. the maintenance of satisfaction to a customer. However, other value formulae than profit formulae have become very popular — even more popular than profit — these days to business especially as a reaction to e.g. the financial crisis and the global heating.

From these acknowledged academic works, we found some generic dimensions that support the idea that any business could be defined by such generic dimensions.

4.1. *Value proposition dimension*

All business models we checked in our research (Appendix 1) acknowledge that any business offers values. We define these as value proposition offered to the customers or users. This can be in the form of products, services and/or process of services and products (Appendix 6 Table7). Values are offered by the business as related to the *customer functions* that the business offers to solve for the customer (Abell 1983). Customer values can be products — a light bubble, services — an installation of a lamp or solutions to a specific lighting to a building or a value proposition process — a specific process consisting of lamps, installation and lighting through a certain time period delivered in a certain process to the customer. Kotler (1983) supports this argument by expressing that any business delivers or offers values in a form as products and/or services and/or process. (Magretta 2002, Osterwalder 2002, 2012, Johnson 2008, Chesbrough 2008, Casadesus-Masanell 2010, Teece 2010, Zott 2010).

The literature of business process engineering (Hammer 1990, Davenport 1990) increases the value proposition dimension as it argues for a value proposition process and this is further supported by Chan (Chan 2008) talking about a value proposition process before, under and after a certain value proposition exchange is carried out. A value proposition process hereby takes in the time aspect of any value proposition exchange and extends the value proposition offer from any business to more than just products and/or services.

4.2. *Customers and/or User dimension*

All academia and practitioners we checked agree that business serves customers or/and users (Appendix 1). "*A successful* business *is one that has found a way to create value for its customers — that has found* "a way" *to help customers* or/and *to get an important job done* (Johnson 2008). "*It's not possible to invent or reinvent a business model without first identifying a clear customer value proposition"* (Johnson 2008).

Here, we draw a distinction between customers and users. Customers pay with money — " *there is no marked* – Business – *if the customers do not pay"* (Kotler 1983), whereas users (von Hippel 2005) do not pay with anything or pay with other values.

Business Model theory (Appendix 1) until now has only considered the business model related to customers. However, as we will see later and as von Hippel argued users can be highly valuable to business by "paying" with other values.

4.3. *Value Chain Functions [Internal Part] dimension*

Any operating business has functions which are (Porter 1996, Sanchez 1996, 2000) able to "offer" value propositions and serve the customers and/or users with values. Most of the academia frameworks we checked acknowledge this but few are very concrete about which functions and some have not even mentioned these.

A value chain function list could be adapted from Porters Value Chain framework (Porter 1985, 1996) including primary functions — inbound logistics, operation, out bound logistics, marketing and sales, service — and support functions — procurement, human resource management, administration and finance infrastructure, business model innovation. We changed Porter's product and technology development support function to a broader support function, which we call Business Model Innovation function, as we believe that BMI covers Porter's two support functions. The BMI function was not

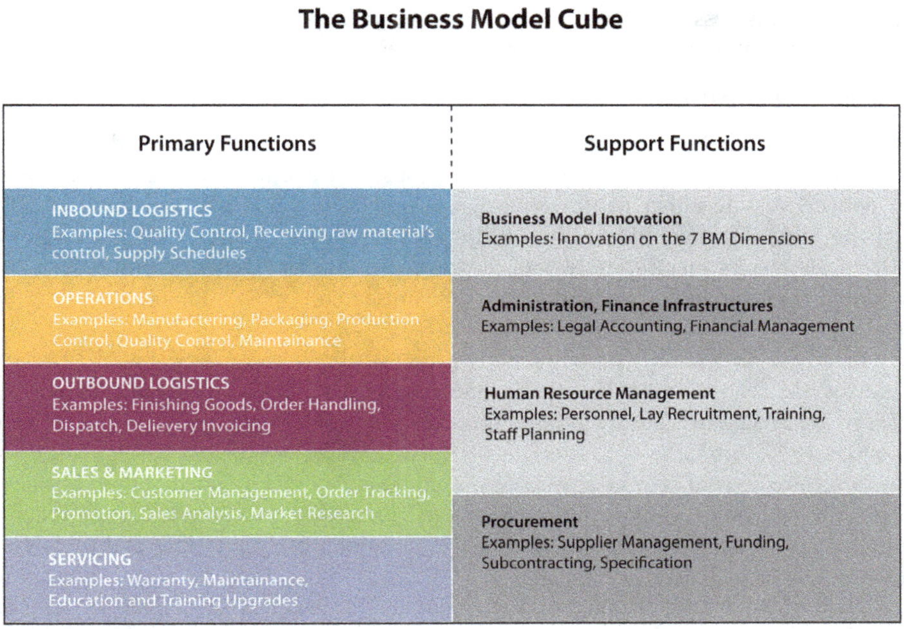

The Business Model Cube

Primary Functions	Support Functions
INBOUND LOGISTICS Examples: Quality Control, Receiving raw material's control, Supply Schedules	**Business Model Innovation** Examples: Innovation on the 7 BM Dimensions
OPERATIONS Examples: Manufactering, Packaging, Production Control, Quality Control, Maintainance	**Administration, Finance Infrastructures** Examples: Legal Accounting, Financial Management
OUTBOUND LOGISTICS Examples: Finishing Goods, Order Handling, Dispatch, Delievery Invoicing	**Human Resource Management** Examples: Personnel, Lay Recruitment, Training, Staff Planning
SALES & MARKETING Examples: Customer Management, Order Tracking, Promotion, Sales Analysis, Market Research	
SERVICING Examples: Warranty, Maintainance, Education and Training Upgrades	**Procurement** Examples: Supplier Management, Funding, Subcontracting, Specification

Figure 2 Value Chain functions — primary and secondary function list of any BM.

considered by Porter at the time he introduced the Value Chain Model. Porter was, at that time, primarily focusing on products and the activities of the value chain. We propose the list of Value Chain Functions [Internal Part seen in Figure 2] to be carried out in any BM.

Any operating business needs to have some of these functions in some degrees — which Porter refers to as activities that are carried out to enable a business function and be able to fulfill its purpose — either by itself or carried out by others. The result of carrying out these functions is value added and/or less costs (Porter 1996) which can be proposed as value propositions.

Porters list was originally described as activities and developed on the background of an operating business. It was not particularly made for "TO BE" business — entrepreneurs, new or changed business and business that was in a "phase of BMI" before market introduction or made ready for operation. Our model acknowledges "AS IS" activities but we find that it is necessary to include also the functions of a "TO BE" BM that is not yet operating and have activities.

4.4. Competences dimension

Very few BM frameworks comment and address the questions — How are the activities and functions carried out? Who takes care of the value chain functions? According to Prahalad and Hamel (Prahalad 1990), any business can have competences but only few businesses would have core competences. According to Prahalad and Hammel, competences can be divided in four groups — technology, human resource, organizational system and culture. Technology covers product-, production- and process technologies, human resources cover the employees used in the business, organizational system and culture of the business (Tillich 1951, 1990). The business can choose either to use own competences or network partners competences to carry out the values chain functions.

4.5. Network dimension

Håkonson argued that any business is in a network of other businesses and thereby *"no Business is an Island"* (Håkonsson 1990). Any business is a network-based business and these networks could either be physical, digital or/and virtual (Child and Faulkner 1995, Goldmann 1998, Hammel 2001, Choi 2003, Vervest 2005, Lindgren 2011). Very few of the BM frameworks mention networks, however, historically networks have been more important and visible in the latest 10 years of BM research.

4.6. Relation dimension

Businesses are related through tangible and intangible relations (Provan 1983, Provan 2007, Provan 2008, Alee 2011,) to other businesses customers, competences and networks (Håkonson 1990, Amidon 2008, Russels 2012). Businesses are related through strong and weak ties (Granovettar 1973) Businesses send value propositions to other businesses through relations and receive value propositions from other businesses through relations. Relations can be one to one or one to many. Relations can be visible and invisible to humans or machines (Lindgren 2012).

Tangible and intangible relations are used in the business to deliver values (Alee 2011). Businesses relate their value proposition, users/customers, value chain functions, competences and network through relations. Relations are used for creating, capturing, delivering, receiving and consuming values. Value propositions are sent through tangible and intangible relations to users, customers, competences and network. Relations are connected to roles (Alee 2011) either played by customers, competences or/and network partners.

Very few BM frameworks include relations. Osterwalder (Osterwalder 2011) acknowledges customer relations as the business is related to customers but seems to forget relations to suppliers and other stakeholders in the BM. Only very few (Casadesus-Masanell 2010, Alee 2011) go into visualizing and documenting value transfers through relations in BM. We found that a BM without relations between the other BM dimensions will never be able to operate and become an "AS IS" BM.

4.7. Value formula dimension

Any business uses some kind of a formula to calculate the value it offers to the business, market, industry and/or the world. Very few BM frameworks comment on this formula and those who do are quiet blurred about the formulae.

The value formula is a formula that shows how the value and the cost are calculated by the business (Henry 1978, Kotler 1983, Porter 1985, Osterwalder 2002). The result of this calculation is a value formulae either expressed in money or/and other values. Henry talks about a profit maximization formula, Kotler talks about several pricing models, Porter discusses different competitive pricing formulas and Osterwalder (Osterwalder 2011) expressed this in his BM framework it as revenue and cost structure. Very few academia dealing with BM deal with how the business calculates the value they want to get out of the BM.

Several authors have documented that any business operates and is influenced by its business environment — external. In this paper, we leave the political, economic, social, technical, environmental, legal (PESTEL 2007) conditions and competitive (Porter 1980) contexts and environment dimensions for further comments although we acknowledge that the business environment is critical to the business.

The above mentioned seven dimensions are equivalent to the overall model we propose of how any business is constructed. The seven dimensions seen in Table 2 should be considered by any business that is interested in running its operations well. However, there is a difference between the way businesses want to run their operations — seven visionary dimensions of a business and how a business really runs its operations. By mapping empirical data from our business case studies to the seven dimensions, we found that most businesses have more than one business model. In other words, the businesses they described via the seven dimensions are different to how they actually run their business models. Some of these business models were close to their original description of the seven dimensions but others were different.

This places our attention to the fact that businesses could potentially have more business models and that there could exist a level beneath the level of the business's overall dimensions. We therefore address the importance of investigation of the business models and draw a distinction between a visionary model of a business and the models of business that are actually carried out (AS IS) and are intended to be carried out (TO BE) in the business.

Most academics working with BMs have until now covered the term BM at the business level and at the visionary level. Further, they cover it as just one BM for any business as seen in Table 1.

This observation together with inspiration from Abell´s and Hamel' original definitions and framework of "The core Business" (Abell 1983), "The core competence" (Hamel 1995) made us adapt the definition of "the core business model" as the BM model at a business level and business visionary level, which states how businesses related to the seven dimensions may wish to run their businesses.

The core business model refers to: "How a business wants to construct and intends to operate its "main" and "essential" business related to the seven business dimensions — value proposition, user and/or customer groups, value chain [internal functions], competence, network, relations and value formula."

The business Model refers to: "How a certain business model in the business is constructed actually operates — "AS IS" BM — or is intended to be constructed — "TO BE" BM related to the seven dimensions — value proposition, user and/or customer Groups, value chain [internal functions], competence, network, relations and value formula"

In our research, we found that businesses do not stick strictly to their core business and how they want their Business Model to look like and be. They have in fact a variety and a mix of BMs with different value propositions, users and customers, value chains with different functions, competences, network, relations and value formulas. One set of dimensions do not fit all business models, markets, industries, worlds (Lindgren 2011). These mix of dimensions — which we classify as different business models exist and coexists within the core business — what we call BMs inside the business as illustrated in Figure 3 — but also exists and coexists outside the business. Individual BMs are not necessarily aligned strictly to the core business model and the seven dimensions. All of them have their own specific seven dimensions.

Table 1 Business Model Definition focal points

Author's	BM as framework	BM at Business level	BM at Business Model level
Abell 1980		X	
Timmers (1998)	X		
Venkatraman and Henderson (1998)	X		
Selz (1999)		X?	
Stewart and Zhao, 2000		X	
Linder and Centrell (2000)		X	
Hamel (2000)	X		
Petrovic et al. (2001)		X?	
Weill and Vitale (2001)		X	
Magretta (2002)		X	
Amit and Zott(2002)	X		
Lai, Weill and Malone (2006)		X	
Chesbrough (2007)	X	X	
Skarzynski and Gibson (2008)		X	
Johnson, Hagemann and Christensen 2008	X		
Casadesus-Mansanell and Ricarct (2010)		X	
Johnson (2010)		X	
Osterwalder and Pigneour (2010)		X	
Teece (2010)	X		
Zott		X	
Fielt (2011)		X	

Note: We had difficulties in placing X? precisely due to a kind of fuzziness about what they really mean and focus about. Therefore, their placement is our indication of where they should be.

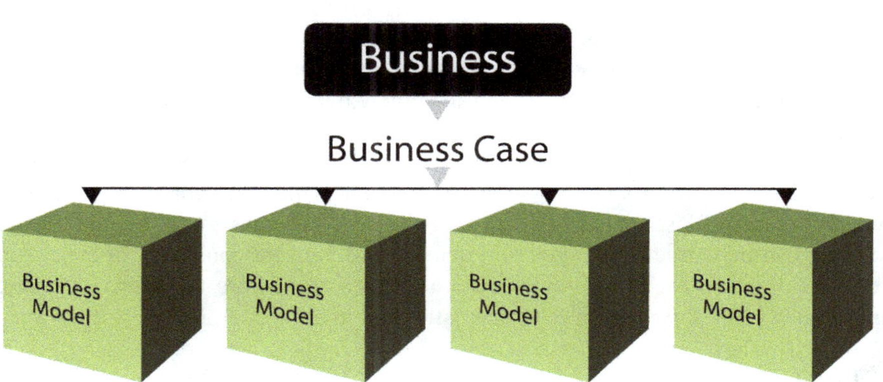

Figure 3 The Multi Business Model approach related to different Business cases.

Table 2 Generic dimensions of a BM

	Core questions related to BM
Core Building Block	Dimensions in the BM
Value Proposition/s (Products, Services and Processes) that the Business offers (Physical, Digital, Virtual)	What are our value propositions?
Customer/s and Users (Target users, Customers, Market Segments that the Business serves – Geographies, Physical, Digital, Virtual).	Who do we serve?
Value Chain [Internal] Configuration.(Physical, Digital, Virtual)	What value chain functions do we provide?
Competences (Assets, Processes and Activities) that translate Business's inputs into value for customers and/or users (outputs). (Physical, Digital, Virtual)	What are our competences?
Network - Network and Network partners (Strategic partners, Suppliers and others (Physical, Digital, Virtual)	What are our networks?
Relations(s) e.g. Physical, Digital and Virtual relations, Personal. (Physical, Digital, Virtual)	What are our relations?
Value Formula (Profit Formulae and other value formulae. (Physical, Digital, Virtual)	What are our value formulae?

We argue therefore that a business's different business models cannot be explained by just one business model — "the core business model" — but would with preference be better explained by different business models — however, still each would have seven generic dimensions, but with different characteristics. In our research, we only found Casadesus-Masanell (Casadesus-Masanell 2010) and to some extent Markides (Markides 2004) who indicates the existence of more BMs in a business.

As a consequence, we propose that a business can be said to have one or more BMs related to different business cases — the multi-business model approach (Lindgren 2011) — which are more, less or not aligned with the core business model. However, any of these BMs can be defined as related to a generic BM concept consisting of seven generic dimensions. Each of the seven dimensions addresses some core questions in relation to each individual BM´s dimensions characteristics and logic.

5. The BM Component level

Each BM dimension can be divided into components (Appendix 6 Table 7). We now exemplify the business model dimensions by explaining how each dimension in any business model can be different and how they can be characterized on a BM component level. The level of detail of each dimension is up to the individual business to decide. Business can "dive" as deep in detail as it wishes, however, our research shows that it must give meaning to the business to go in detail. Businesses must be able to get value out of the details, otherwise they will miss the overview and motivation of mapping their Business Models.

5.1. The Value proposition dimension component level — What value propositions do the BM provide? — (VP)

The definition of value (Alderson, 1957; Drucker, 1973; Albrecht, 1992; Anderson, 1982; Woodruff, 1997; Anderson, 1999; Doyle, 2000; Lindgreen 2005, Wouters, 2005, Chan 2005, Osterwalder, 2005 *et al.*) is manifold and its development since the 1950s during the "era of innovation" has been covered intensely in academia.

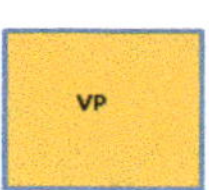

The Value chain dimension.

Value (Albretcht, 1992; Alderson, 1957; Anderson, 1982; Anderson and Narus, 1999; Doyle, 2000; Drucker, 1973; Woodruff, 1997; Lindgreen, 2005) is key in understanding the value of a product, service, process and relationship offered. However, value proposition varies related to different customers, because just as customers are different they are also satisfied by different values whether it is from products, services, a relationship or a value fulfillment delivered in a process by products and services (Lindgren 2011). "Managers today continuously ask themselves: How can we understand customer's value and how can we deliver "real" value to customers in a cost efficient and profitable way?" (Johnston 2008).

The customer´s value equation is often very complex to understand in detail because it is not static but dynamic over time (Lingreen 2005). Therefore, value proposition has to be understood from the perspective of the customer and/or user it is delivered to, by the context it is delivered in, the time it is delivered and the place it is delivered.

Value can be said to be closely connected to the concept of "total value and cost to the customer" (Wouters, Andersson, and Wynstra, 2005). In this case, staying at the point of entry to a trade or a value proposition process is strongly related to the customer´s total perceived value and total perceived cost related to the products, services or process. This is why it is incredibly difficult as a business to measure, read the values and cost of a customer, and to decide the degree of attractiveness of a value — or if a value is judged high or low related to a trade or a process. In this paper, we focus on what the business — or business model believe it offers related to value — the business viewpoint (Lindgren 2011). However, we acknowledge there are other views of a value.

The solution to classifying value proposition taken by many businesses is to offer different value propositions to different customers, which argues that value proposition offered by a business is often different to each **customer, context, time** and **place**.

Payne and Holt (1999) outline four types of values related to values.

1. **Use Values** — the properties and qualities, which accomplish a use, work, or service for the customer
2. **Esteem Value** — the properties, features, or attractiveness, which causes a want to own the product and service for the customer
3. **Cost Value** — the sum of labor, materials, and various other cost required to produce it for the customer
4. **Exchange Value** — its properties or qualities, which enable exchanging it for something else that the customer wants

We found that this list of types of values had to be complemented by an overall dimension of work time vs. lifetime (Fogh Kirkeby, 2007). Time as the factor that is defining customers personal or business values of the e.g. trade or process is related to an overall lifetime value and describes the sum of actions taken in order to find work life-fulfilling and transcend oneself, a value often seen as the driver of projects, art etc (Tillich 1951, Austin 2005, Sandberg 2007 *et al.*).

Value also has to be measured **before, under** and **after** value exchange has taken place (Chan 2005). This means that a customer could trade or collaborate on the value from a product and service that comes out of the trade (Kotler 1984, Ziethaml, 1988; Doyle, 2000) but also from the value of the relationship (Reichheld, 1993; Lindgreen and Wynstra, 2005). The creation, capturing, delivering, receiving and consumption of value through a relationship (Brodie, Brookes and Coviello, 2000; Lindgreen, 2001; Danaher and Johnston, 2002; Lindgreen, Antioco and Beverland, 2003, Lindgren 2012) is the value equation of an inter-organizational collaboration project — a network-based BM. This is one important value and also an attraction factor, which could be in this case, an innovation of a "TO BE" business model. The value of this can be other than money e.g. learning. Please see a list of non-monetary values in Appendix 2.

This is in line with research claiming that the value of the relationship, activity links, resource ties, and actor's bonds (Axelsson and Easton, 1992; Håkonsson, 1982; Håkonsson and Snehota, 1995; Ford, 2001; Ford et al., 2002; Ford et al., 2003) can be even more important than the value of the product or service. The value of the relationship is both an input but also an output of the business model innovation process, which supports the argument that value is not static but dynamic.

As values are created, captured, delivered, received and consumed in a value process, they are continuously undergoing change throughout the business model innovation process or the life time of values. Values of relationship can be related directly (e.g. profit, volume-, safeguard-functions) both also indirectly (e.g. innovation-, market-, scout-, access-functions). The value functions (Walter, 2001) can further be of a low and/or high performing character (Lindgreen and Wynstra, 2005) which is often up to the customer´s judgment and to influence the degree of this value. Chan and Maubourgne (Chan 2005) express this in their strategic value map Appendix 3. However, their value map is just seen from the business view point and not from the customers or other view points (Lindgren 2011).

The value of a customer should also be understood as perceived value — benefits and cost (Woodroff, 1997; Walter, 2001; Lindgren, 2002), which means that the real value of a product, service and/or a process can in some cases be neglected in advance to a higher or lower perceived value of a product, service or a process. Furthermore, perceived value should not just be related only to the individual customer but also to other individuals as other customers, users (von Hippel 2005), competences (technology, humans, organizational systems and culture), network (suppliers, other network) in the business model interpretation of the product, service and/or process. (Blois, 2004) Therefore, it is the user's, customer´s, competencies, network´s interpretation of "value" that is important and not just what the business and its stakeholders (investors, the market, the business, the innovation leader) think ought to be or are the values — that is the real value proposition of the BM.

It is therefore important when analyzing and understanding a product, service and/or process value, to analyze all stakeholders and both values and perceived values. Furthermore, it is important to analyze value and perceived value over time, during the trade or inter-organizational collaborative process, as both values and perceived value are dynamic and will therefore by definition always change throughout the entire value process and thereby over time. Today, no business model framework has managed to and is able to cover and capture value change over time.

Values can be tangible and/or intangible. Tangible is something you can see, touch or feel and others can get a full view of these items. Intangible is "something" you cannot see, touch or feel physically.

We make a distinction between the tangible and intangible values and associated value objects: tangibles and intangibles values. Tangible value objects have often a direct financial value, underpinned by an accepted financial marketplace for realizing the value.

A view to tangible and intangible value view is taken by Verna Allee [All 2008] who defines tangible values as tangible deliverables to include anything that is contracted, mandated or expected by the recipient as part of the delivery of a product, service or/and a process that directly generates revenue. Intangible value objects, as proposed by Allee, could be considered in three main groups:

- Intangibles where a financial market may be established but where the stability and absolute nature of the value may be questionable (such as intellectual property).
- Intangibles where a measure is established with a wide acceptance of the measurement approach (carbon footprint).

- Intangibles where only a specific context is applicable with values very much related to that context.

Li draws a comparison between tangibles and intangibles in relation to markets and contexts (Li 2012). This enables us to include the operation of social businesses/exchanges within this definition of tangibles and intangibles.

In summary, any business model may offer a value proposition which can be offered as tangible and/or intangible value. Value proposition can be products, services and/or processes of product and services. Value propositions can be values of relations.

5.2. Customers and Users dimension component level — Who does the BM serve? (CU)

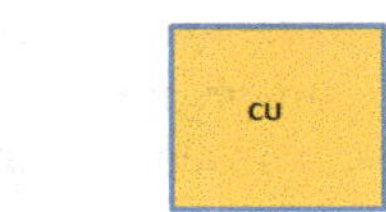

The Customer and User dimension

Any business model that we researched talks about business models having customers. However, we found that many BMs do not have customers that pay for BM´s value proposition, but are constructed around users, which provide the foundation for other BMs with customers. Facebook, Skype, Linkin, Twitter and Google are examples of such business models.

Our research showed that BMs built upon users, when growing big in numbers of users, can attract and activate customers willing to buy — or pay for value propositions in other BMs. Either users start to pay for better performance, advanced use, deeper content e.g. or other customers buy e.g. promotion because there are so many users in the BM. In these cases, the customers pay for other or different value propositions — or a different BM — as the users. Stock buyers of Facebook business could be an example. The customers, however, can also at the same time be users of the value offering in the user-based BM. Stock buyers of Facebook business are probably also Facebook users. Thereby, customers can play different roles in a BM and in different BM´s.

This is also one of the arguments why we point to the existence of more BMs (Lindgren 2012, Lindgren 2013) in any business where our research shows that BMs are often interrelated and add value and influence to each other.

We therefore propose to distinguish between users and customers by defining users as not paying for the value proposition (Kotler 1983, Von Hippel 2005) while customers pay for the value proposition (Kotler 1983).

Users can, however, "pay" with other value, other value transfers and thereby contribute to development of very important values for other business models. These values could be learning for future BMI, development of critical user mass that would be attractive for other BMs, change of general market context and direction. Needless to say, there can be many other valuable contributions from user-based BMs to customer-based BMs (Appendix 3).

5.3. Value Chain functions [Internal] dimension component level — What value chain functions do the BM have? — (VC)

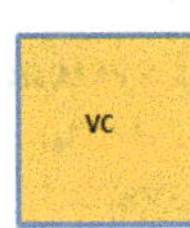

The Value Chain function Dimension

Any business model must carry out certain activities to prod uce the value proposition to the users and/or customers. A list of these activities was proposed by Michael Porter in his value chain framework (Porter 1985). Porter called for these activities and proposed some primary activities and some secondary activities of a value chain. A value chain was proposed by Porter to include one or all of these activities, however, if some activities were missing and not carried out, our research shows that this can stop the BM's operations or that the BM will never come to operate in the business and the market.

Porter's Value Chain framework was related to an operating BM. However, when businesses commence to create a "TO BE" BM there are really no active activities, just wish and expectation of value chain functions the BM should carry out. Further, when we observe an operating business at a certain moment — in this case, we freeze the picture of a specific BM — we do not see "running" activities but just functions that are carried out (Appendix 4). Value chain functions in our BM framework represent the value chain functions that have to be carried out or are being carried out within the BM. We acknowledge that there are value chain functions outside the BM but in this paper we only focus on the internal value Chain functions of the BM.

5.4. Competence dimension component level — What are the BM's competences? — (C)

Any business model relies on and uses competences, either from the focal business, from network partners or even from customers and users to carry out the value chain functions to create, capture, deliver, receive and consume the value propositions.

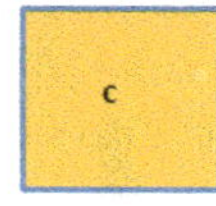

The Competence dimension

According to Prahalad and Hammel,(Prahalad 1990) competences can be divided to four main categories according to Prahalad and Hammel Technologies, HR, Organizational Structure and culture.

Technologies according to (Sanchez 1996, 2000, 2001) we divided into

1. Product- and service-technologies
2. Production technology — both "Product- and Service-production technologies"
3. Process technology — process technologies that run and steer the production technologies so that the product and service technologies can be created, captured, delivered, received and consumed.

Each BM has a specific mix, integration and use of product- and service- technologies, production technologies and process technologies. Some mix, integration and use of technologies are so unique that the competence can be a core competence (Prahalad and Hammel).

Human Resources are the people — either white collar or blue collar (Peters xxxx) that the BM can use to carry out the Value Chain functions. The human resource, the mix and the use of human resource can also be so unique that human resource too is rendered as a core competence.

Organizational system is the system that the business models use to organize the use of technologies and human resource to carry out the Value Chain functions. The organizational system can also be so unique that the organizational system is a core competence.

Culture is the "soft" part of the competence dimension. We claim that any BM has a specific culture. The culture can be adapted one to one from the business or other BMs but can also be incremental even radically different to these.

5.5. Network — What are the BM's networks?

Any business model is a network-based BM. No BM is a lonely island — at least not for very long time. Why? — because if a BM does not receive value from outside it will slowly shrink and vanish. If it does not offer a value proposition of any kind it will not be able to receive value in a long time perspective. The BM network hereby becomes vital to any BM — a BM is its network.

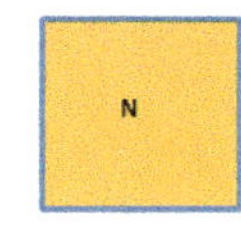

The Network dimension

Networks can be physical networks (Håkonson 1990), digital networks (Choi 2003) or/and virtual networks (Coldmann and Price 2005, Vervest 2005) that the BMs use.

5.6. Relations dimension component level — What are the BM's relations? — (R)

Any Business Model relies on relations. In our research, we found four sets of relations that are of importance to BMs (Appendix 4) and should be attended to by business managers as shown in Figure 4.

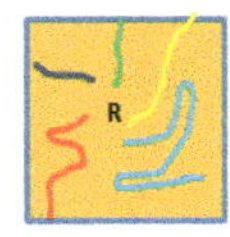

The Relation dimension

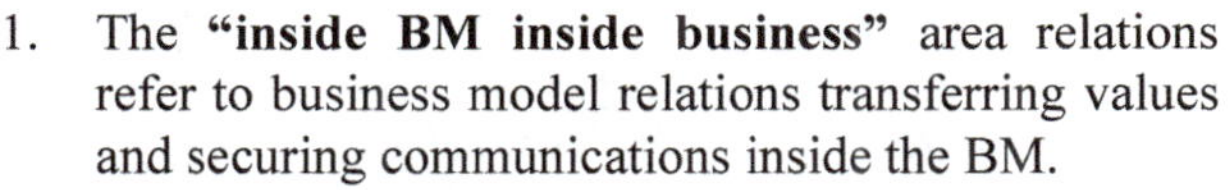

1. The **"inside BM inside business"** area relations refer to business model relations transferring values and securing communications inside the BM.

2. The **"inside business outside BM"** area refers to relations between different BMs inside the business.

3. The **"inside BM outside business"** refers to relations between BMs outside of the business.

4. The **"Outside BM Outside business"** refers to relations and relation area where the BM and business do not share a relation.

Value and values of a BM can be seen in a broader perspective as each partner's BM's relation to users, customers, competences, networks in the inter-organizational network of relations to "AS IS" and "TO BE" BM's. Why? Because value and cost are strongly interrelated with relationships (Blois, 2004), and attributes related to the relationship between the partners BMs in e.g. a simple trade "AS IS" BM or an BM innovation project "TO BE" BM where goods and services are not necessarily defined. Needless to say, these relations influence each other and are interrelated.

As was seen earlier, value equation is not only related to products, services and processes but is also strongly connected to the relations and thereby a result of the relation between BMs in either a trade or an innovation project. Value equation can be related to irrespective of whether the BMs are related or not. In this paper, we only cover the internal relations — the "In In" relations — in a BM.

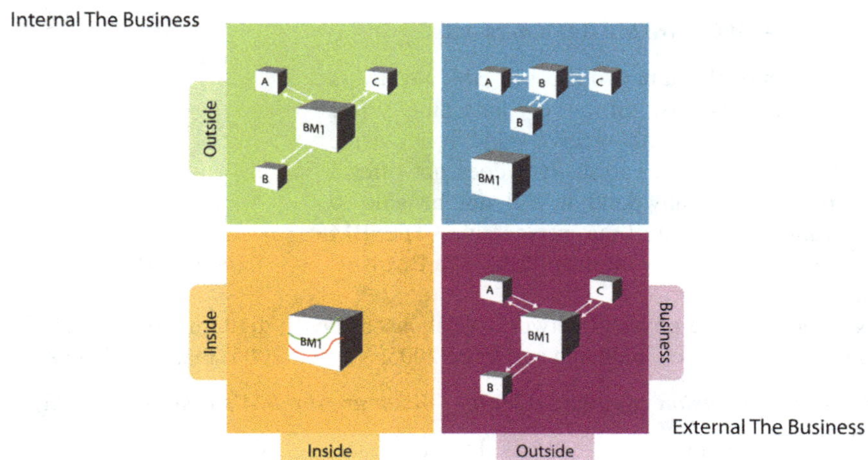

Figure 4 The Relations areas related to a BM – The Relation Axiom Lindgren and Horn Rasmussen 2012.

Relations, activity links, resource ties, and actor's bonds (Axelsson and Easton, 1992; Håkonsson, 1982; Håkonsson and Snehota, 1995; Day 2000; Ford, 2001;Ford *et al*., 2002; Ford et al., 2003) are all tools used to describe and map relations.

The creation, capturing, delivering, receiving and consumption of value is enabled through relations (Brodie, Brookes and Coviello, 2000; Lindgreen, 2001; Danaher and Johnston, 2002; Lindgreen, Antioco and Beverland, 2003, Lindgren 2012). Relations connect the different BM dimensions' components and enable the creation, capturing, delivering, receiving and consumption process of value. However, if any BM is not able or willing to send and receive the value through the relations, then the relation has no value and no task.

5.7. Value formula dimension component level — What are the BM's value formulae? — (VF)

Any business model will have one or more value formulae, which can be expressed in either a monetary and/or in a nonmonetary value formulae. The term profit formula as a dimension in a BM that we found through our research has to be changed to a dimension called the value formula dimension to cover all BMs. We found that the term profit formula is too narrow a terminology to express the formula by which any BM calculates the value of a BM. Our research showed that many businesses and BMs are not focused, or are not exclusively focused on profit but instead on other value formulae. They "calculate" on other value formulae and to get a full understanding of why business models exist and are

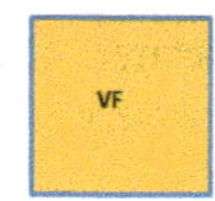

The Value formula dimension

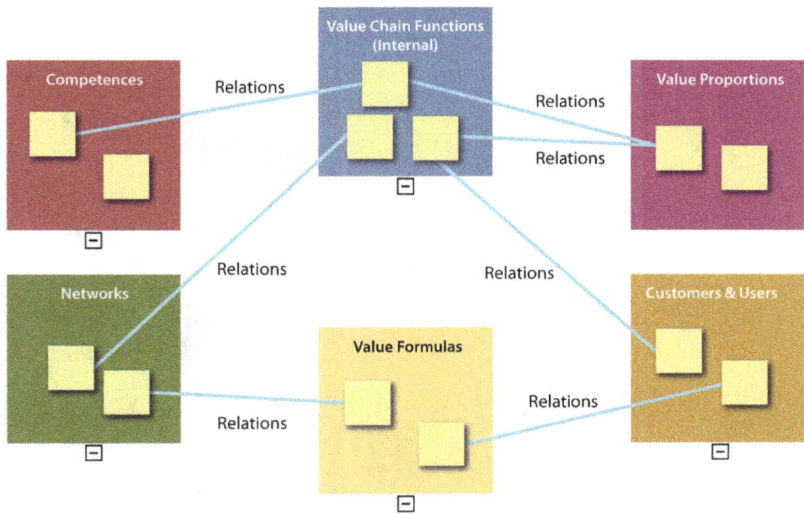

Figure 5 The seven dimensions of the Business Model cube in a 2D presentation.

innovated it is necessary to include other values. We therefore propose profit formula as one of many value formulae that can be the "calculated" output of a BM. However, we claim that any BM has one or more calculated value formulae — monetary and/or non-monetary. A BM can have more than one value formulae.

Having verified academically that the seven dimensions of the BM exists, it enables us to complete the concept of the BM Cube. In a 2D picture and with the seven dimensions spread out flat it would look like Figure 5.

However, we discovered that the seven dimensions form a BM Cube with the "IN IN" relations inside the Cube as shown in a sketch model in Figure 6.

The 2D version is very helpful when working on a BM dimension level and the 3D version are helpful when working on a BM, BM portfolio, business and BM ecosystem level. Both presentations are helpful when working on BMI, see Table 3.

Figure 6 The seven dimensions of the Business Model cube presentation.

Table 3 An example of a portfolio of BM´s in the KB use case (Lindgren 2013)

KB BM Case

Business

Business Case

Business Models

	KB Lottery Business Model	KB Cancer Disease Business Model	KB Cancer Information Business Model	KB Cancer Patient Support Business Model
Core Building Block	Building Block	Building Block	Building Block	Building Block
Value proposition/s (Products, Services and Processes) that the company offers (Physical, Digital, Virtual)	Lottery, possibility to win money, things and services	Research aimed at Fighting Cancer disease	Development of Information material aimed discovering and Fighting Cancer disease at an early stage, preventative	Developing and running Cancer Patient Support
Users and Customer/s (Target users, Customers, Market segments that the company Serves geographies, Physical, Digital, Virtual)	Donator who wants to support research in cancer, support of cancer patients, information about cancer	Donator who wants to support fight of Cancer Disease	Donator who wants to support development of information about Cancer Disease	Donator who wants to support development and running Cancer Patient Support
Value Chain (Internal) configuration. (Physical, Digital, Virtual)	KB value chain functions necessary to run the KB lottery	KB value chain functions necessary to handle funding support for cancer research	KB value chain functions necessary to handle information about cancer research, cancer patient support activities, cancer discovery and protection	KB value chain functions necessary to handle Cancer Patient Support
Competencies (Assets, Processes and Activities) that translate company's inputs into value for customers (Outputs). (Physical, Digital, Virtual)	KB technology, HR, organisational structure and culture included in the KB Lottery	KB technology, HR, organisational structure and culture included in the KB cancer research funding handling	KB technology, HR, organisational structure and culture included in the KB cancer information activities and handling	KB technology, HR, organisational structure and culture included in the KB Cancer Patient Support activities and handling
Network - Network and Network partners (e.g. Strategic partnerships, supply chains and others (Physical, Digital, Virtual)	KB network partners involved in the KB lottery	KB network partners involved in the cancer research funding BM	KB network partners involved in the cancer information activities	KB network partners involved in the Cancer Patient Support activities
Relation(s), Relationship(s) (e.g. Physical, Digital, Virtual relations, personal, peers) (Physical, Digital, Virtual)	KB relations inside the KB lottery BM	KB relations inside the KB research funding BM	KB relations inside the KB information	KB relations inside the KB Cancer Patient Support BM
Value Formula (Profit formula - Both turnover structure, Cost structure and revenge floe and other value formula.) (Physical, Digital, Virtual)	Price of lottery - cost of developing and running the KB Lottery	Price of newspaper - cost of developing, running and distributing the KB research cancer funding	BM Price of KB information - cost of developing, running and distributing the KB information BM	BM Price of KB information - cost of developing and running KB Cancer Patient Support BM

6. Discussion

Today, most academia's and practitioners consider the BM as measurable, objective and one of a kind. Although there are many different definitions (Taran 2011) and types of business models (e.g., open and closed business models (Chesbrough 2007, Lindgren 2011), free business models (Anderson 2009), internet-based business models (Zott 2002), most define business model at a business level and at a core business level (Abell 1983). We propose that there is a need for a distinction between levels of business model focus as proposed in tabel 4. The business level — the core business model and the business models existing under the "umbrella" of the core business model. This is to prevent fuzziness and support discussion and further development of the BM theory.

Tabel 4 Levels of Business Model

Levels of Business Model	Characteristics of the BM level
BM component The Smallest part of a BM dimension	**Value proposition components** Value attitudes, attributes **Customer and User** customer and User roles **Value chain functions** Primary functions: Inbound logistics, operation, out bound logistics, Marketing and Sales, Service Support Functions: Procurement, Human Resource Management, Administration, finance infrastructure, Business Model Innovation **Competence** Product-, Production-, and Process Technologies HR – employees/people Organizational System Culture **Network** Physical, digital and virtual network **Relations** **Value formulae** Links, connectors
BM dimension	**Value proposition** **Customer and or User** **Value Chain Functions [Internal]** **Competence** **Network** **Relations** **Value formulae**
BM	**BM Cube** with the seven dimensions — "TO BE" or "AS IS" BM Cube — 2D and 3D presentation
BM portfolio	**Group of BM Cubes** that are interrelated
Business	**The core Business** level with seven dimensions
Business Model ecosystem	**A BM ecosystem** where businesses BM are bid.

Some BMs together can form a group of BM that is interrelated — what we call a portfolio(s) of BMs in the business (Lindgren 2011). These BMs form a group of BMs that have similarities due to e.g. the same customer focus, use of the same value chain, use of the same network. Often the BM portfolio´s BMs are interdependent. As earlier mentioned, some BMs attract users who attract customers to other BMs in the BM portfolio. An example of this is shown by the case study of KB (Lindgren 2012).

Further, we consider every business to be part of one or more business model ecosystems. BM's ecosystem is where the business BMs operate and "exchange" its value proposition e.g. manure BM Ecosystem in the Vlastuin case, healthcare sector in the HSJD case (Appendix 4).

We propose that business models and BMI should be viewed on different levels as shown in Table 4.

Businesses are doing BMI at different business model levels. The BM ecosystem level is considered as being the most complex level of BMI. The BM Cube can be considered valuable at all levels. BM Cube can be useful for BMs "on the way to the market" ("TO BE" BM´s) and on BMs "already in the market" ("AS IS" BM´s). It is possible to "innovate", "measure", "test" and "see" when any "BM cube". It is possible to see if the BM is finished and how and why it is functioning or not functioning. It is possible to see the BM cube and its dimensions and components at different levels.

Summing up from the above mentioned, we propose that any BM cube consists of seven dimensions — six sides and the BM relations in the BM — inside the BM cube that binds all other dimensions and components together and enables creation, capturing, delivering, receiving and consumption of values. We illustrate the BM Cube in Figure 7.

7. Business Cases

In order to approach the combination of business and BMs to define the BM cube, two case studies are presented. The first case is based on the Dutch business Vlastuin which is implementing several new "TO BE" BM´s in order to reinforce its business and already has several BMs operating "AS IS" BM´s in order to sustain the business. The second case is concerned with an already functioning hospital HSJD which introduced a whole range of "TO BE" BM´s in relation to the hospitals business.

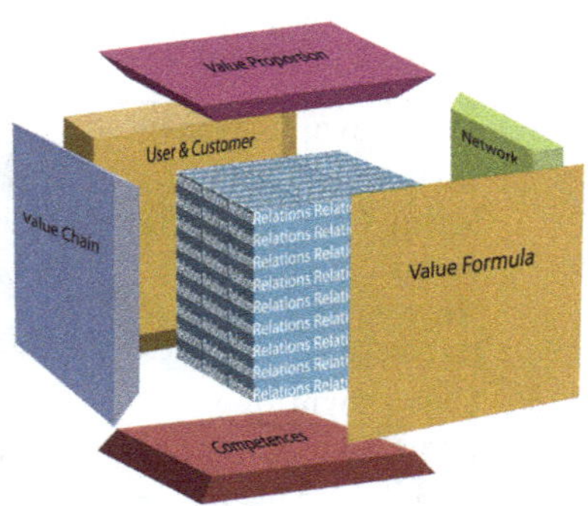

Figure 7 The BM cube.

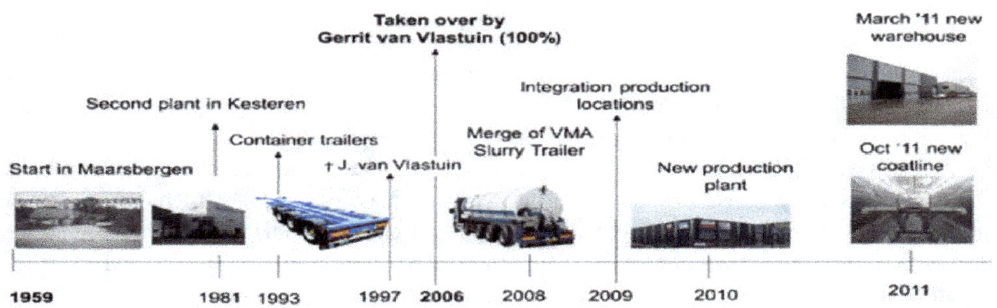

Figure 8 Vlastuin's business evolvement.

Vlastuin (Appendix 4)

Vlastuin started its operations in 1959 and is located in Netherlands. Vlastuin employs around 150 people and had a turnover of 27 million EUR in 2011. During more than 50 years of presence, Vlastuin has added more BMs to its business and thereby slowly increased its core business. It started off by installing and servicing furnaces and boilers, gradually moved to manufacturing to later on adding assembling of cranes and parts to the business. A graphical representation of Vlastuin business evolvement can be seen in Figure 8.

In Appendix 4, a detailed description and analysis of the case is presented.

HSJD Hospital (Appendix 4)

Hospital Sant Joan De Dieu (HSJD) belongs to the Hospital Order of Saint John of God and is a private, non-profit hospital. The order is represented in more than 50 countries and has almost 300 healthcare centers worldwide. HSJD is located in Barcelona, Spain, and is a children and maternity care center. HSJD is a university hospital connected to the University of Barcelona and is also associated with the Hospital Clinic of Barcelona, which helps the hospital to provide top-level technological and human care. HSJD is 95 % financed by the Catalonian public system and the remaining 5% comes from private investments. The primary goal of HSJD is to encourage and educate a healthy lifestyle with good nutrition, proper sleep, hygiene and exercise.

In Appendix 4, a detailed description and analysis of the case is presented.

8. Conclusion

The BM CUBE concept was evolved through our research on top of the increasing business model literature and practice. The BM Cube concept came out of the research and test in the Neffics FP 7 EU project. Today, BM is argued to be a general model for how any business should run its business. Conversely, this paper argues that no business has one Business Model — one model on which they run their business — but businesses have more BMs to conduct businesses. The paper addresses the concern with the difference between the level of a business — the core business — and the level of its business models.

The research addresses further the gap in research and strong demand to find a generic definition and language of a BM. The significance and importance of this work is related to the huge unexplored possibilities that business model innovation offers, when we fully understand the levels, dimensions and components of the business models thoroughly and are able to communicate, work and innovate with business models at these levels. In this context, we proposed that any BM is related to seven dimensions — value proposition, user and/or customer, value chain functions [internal], competence, network, relations, value formulae. The paper also proposes six different levels of a BM from the most detailed level — component to the dimension, BM, BM portfolio, business and business model ecosystem layer. The Vlastuin and HSJD case studies showed the BM Cube framework in practice and verified that the seven dimensions really exist in any BM that we studied in our research.

Conceptually, the BM cube was formed out of the seven dimensions and could be useful both in a 3D and a 2D version. The paper shows how both versions can be useful on different levels.

9. Future Expected Results/Contribution

The study has enlightened a strong demand for testing the BM cube concept in a larger business use case scale and sample. The next step has been initiated a bigger quantitative and qualitative empirical-based research to clarify more details of the BM cube. The tests are intended to be a part of a larger EU and US funded research project together with establishing several BM Cube lab´s.

10. References

[1] Abell, D. F.., “Defining the Business: The Starting Point of Strategic Planning” New Jersey: Prentice-Hall, Inc., 1980.

[2] Alderson, W. (1957) Marketing Behavior and executive action. Homewood, IL: Irwin

[3] Albrecht, K. (1992, November). The Only thing that matters, Executive Excellence, 9, 7.

[4] Anderson, P. (1982), Marketing, Strategic Planning and the theory of the firm. Journal of Marketing, 46 (2), 15 - 26

[5] Anderson, J.C., 6 Narus J.A. (1999) Business Marketing Management Understanding, creating and delivering value. Upper Saddle River, NJ Prentice Hall.

[6] Drucker, 1973; Woodruff, 1997; Doyle, 2000; Lindgreen 2005, Wouters

[7] Allee 2002 Allee V. Value Network Approach http://vernaallee.com/images/VAA-A-ValueNetworkApproach.pdf

[8] Allee 2008 Allee,V. Value Network Analysis and Value Conversion of Tangible and Intangible Assets," Journal of Intellectual Capital. Volume 9 No.1 pp5-24

[9] Allee 2009 Allee V. The Very Human Dynamics of Knowledge and Value Conversion Essays in honour of Professor Karl-Erik Sveiby on his 60th birthday 29th June 2008 http://www.vernaallee.com/images/AlleeChapterSveibyBook-4.pdf

[10] Allee Verna 2010 "Presentation on the OMG 2010 Conference at Santa Clara California US.

[11] Allee Verna and Oliver Schwap 2011 Value networks and the true networks of collaboration Open Source http://www.valuenetworksandcollaboration.com/

[12] Allee 2012 Allee. V Definition of Value Capacity http://valuenetworks.com/public/item/236677

[13] Amidon Debra M. 2008 Innovation SuperHighway Amidon, Debra M Elsevier Science ISBN13: 978-008-049-156-1

[14] Austin, R. & Devin, L. 2004. Artful Making: what managers need to know About how Artists Work Financial Times Prentice Hall.

[15] Blois, K (2004), Analyzing exchanges through the use of value equations The Journal of Business & Industrial Marketing; 2004; 19, 4/5; ABI/INFORM Global

[16] Chan Kim, W. and Mauborgne, R. (2005), Blue Ocean Strategy Harvard Business School Press.

[17] Chesbrough, H. (2007). Open Business Models How to Thrive in the New Innovation Landscape . Harvard Business School .

[18] Child, John; Faulkner, David; Tallmann, Stephan (2005) "Cooperative strategy – Managing Alliances, Networks and Joint Ventures", Oxford University Press

[19] Choi 2003

[20] Coldmann and Price (1995) Agile competition and virtual Organization Van Nordstrand

[21] Daft, R. L. (2010). Understanding the Theory and Design of Organisations. Vanderbilt: South-Western.

[22] Davenport, T. (1990) The new industrial Engineering: Information Technology and Business Process Reenginering. Sloan Management

[23] Day, G.G. (2000). Managing Market Relationships, Journal of the Academy of marketing Science, 28 (1), 24-30

[24] Doyle, P (2000) Value-based Marketing,: marketing strategies for cooperate growth and shareholder value. Chichester. John Wiley and Son.

[25] Drucker, 1973, P (1973) Management: Tasks, responsibilities, practices. New York: Harper Rose.

[26] Fielt, D. E. (2011, March 31 st). Outcomes. Retrieved April 13 th, 2011, from Smart Services CRC: http://www.smartservicescrc.com.au/PDF/Business%20Service%20Management%20 Volume%203.pdf

[27] Kirkeby, O. F. 2000, Management Philosophy - A Radical Normative Perspective Samfundslitteratur, København.

[28] Kirkeby, O. F. 2003, Organisationsfilosofi Samfundslitteratur?, København.

[29] Friedman, T. (November 2007). The World is Flat 3.0. Lecture at Massachusetts Institute of Technology, MIT . Massachusetts, Massachusetts, USA: MIT.

[30] Casadesus-Masanell Ramon and Joan Enric Ricart From Strategy to Business Models and onto Tactics Long Range Planning 43 (2010) 195e215

[31] Fielt, 2011

[32] Granovetter, M. S. 1973, "The Strength of Weak Ties", The American Journal of Sociology, vol. 78, no. 6, pp. 1360-1380.

[33] Goldman, Nagel & Price, 1998, 'Agile Competitors and Virtual Organisations', Van Nostrand Reinhold, New York.

[34] Hammel 2001, Value Network ....

[35] Hammer (1990) Business Process Reengineering work; Don't Automate Obliterate Harvard Business Review July/august

[36] Henry William R. and W. Waren Haynes (1978) Managerial Economics: Analysis and Cases Business Publications, INC. Dallas, Texas

[37] HornGren Charles T. (1977) Cost Accounting A Managerial Emphasis Prentice – Hall, Inc., Englewood Cliffs, N.J. 07632

[38] Håkansson, Håkan & Snehota, I. (1990): No Business is an Island: The Network Concept of Business

[39] Johnson M.W., Christensen, M.C. and Kagermann, H. (2008) Reinventing your business model, Harvard Business Review, vol. 86 No. 12, pp. 50-59

[40] IOT European Commision 2013 http://www.internet-of-things.eu/

[41] Li, Man-Sze et all (2012) Neffics delivery D 3.3. October 2012 – www.neffics.eu

[42] Lambert, D. M., & Cooper, M. C. (2000). Issues in Supply Chain Management. Industrial Marketing Management 29 , 29 (1), 65-83.

[43] Linder, j. and s. cantrell (2000), Changing business models: surfing the landscape, accenture institute for strategic change, canada

[44] Lindgren 2003 Network Based High Speed Product Innovation. PhD Desserteation Center for Industrial production ISBN . Aalborg : Denmark., 2003.

[45] FROM SINGLE FIRM TO NETWORK BASED BUSINESS MODEL INNOVATION. / Lindgren, Peter ; Taran, Yariv ; Boer, Harry International Journal of Entrepreneurship and Innovation Management, Vol. 12, Nr. 2, 03.08.2010, s. 122-137

[46] Lindgren, P. (2011). NEW global ICT-based business models. Aalborg, Denmark: River.

[47] Lindgren, P (2011) BMIL viewpoints – eller Blue ocean paper cinet

[48] Lindgren, P. (2012) Towards a Multi Business Model Innovation Model. / Lindgren, Peter; Jørgensen, Rasmus . Journal of Multi Business Model Innovation and Technology 1 edition River Publisher

[49] Lindgren, P, Morten Karnøe Søndergaard, Mark Nelson and B. J. Fogg (2013) Persuasive Business Models, Journal of Multi Business Model Innovation and Technology, River Publisher

[50] Lindgren, P O. H. Rasmussen and K. F. Saghaug (2013) Business models relations to Intellectual Capital - How to release Intellectual Capital from business BM´s relations? IFKAD Conference Zagreb Croatia Conference Precedings

[51] Kotler, P 1984 Principles of Marketing Prentice Hall

[52] Krcmar Helmut 2011Business Model Research State of the Art and Research Agenda

[53] Magretta J. (2002) " Why Business Models Matter" Harvard Business Review (80:5)

[54] Markides C. & C. Charitou (2004). "Competing dual business models: A contingency approach2, Academy of management executive,. 18(3), pp 22-36

[55] Masanell, R. C., & Ricart, J. E. (2009). From Strategy to Business Model and to Tactics. Hentede 17. May 2012 fra Harvard Business School: http://www.hbs.edu/research/pdf/10-036.pdf

[56] Morris, M.M. Schmindelhutte and J. Allen (2003), The entrepreneur's business model: toward a unified perspective, Journal of business research, 58(6), pp. 726-735.

[57] Neffics 2012 – www.Neffics.eu

[58] Osterwalder, A., Pigneur, Y. and Tucci, L.C. (2004) Clarifying business models: Origins, present, and future of the concept, Communications of AIS, No. 16, pp. 1-25.

[59] Osterwalder, A., Pigneur, Y., & Tucci, C. (Vol. 15. May 2005). Clarifying Business Models. Communications of AIS .

[60] Osterwalder2, A., & Pigneur, Y. (2010). Business Model Generation. New Jersey: John Wiley & Sons, Inc.

[61] Osterwalder 2010 Business-Model-Generation-Visionaries-Challengers

[62] Osterwalder 2011 http://alex.aaltoes.com/

[63] Payne and Holt (1999) Payne, A., & Holt, S. (1999). A review of the dvalueT literature and implications for relationship marketing. Australasian Marketing Journal, 7(1), 41– 51.

[64] Peters Tom (The Innovation Circles

[65] Peng, M. W. (2010). Global. Mason, OH: Sourth-Western.

[66] Porter, M. E. (1985) Competitive Advantage: Creating and sustaining superior performance Harvard Business Review

[67] Porter, M. E. (1996) What is strategy Harvard Business ReviewPorter, M. E. (No. 3. Vol. 79 2001). Strategy and the internet. Harvard Business Review , s. 62-79.

[68] Porter, M (2012), Shared Values Harvard Business Review January 2011

[69] Provan, K. G. 1983, "The Federation as an Interorganizational Linkage Network", The Academy of Management Review, vol. 8, no. 1, p. 79.

[70] Provan, K. G., Fish, A., & Sydow, J. 2007, "Interorganizational Networks at the Network Level: A Review of the Empirical Literature on Whole Networks", Journal of Management, vol. 33, no. 3, pp. 479-516.

[71] Provan, K. G. & Kenis, P. 2008, "Modes of Network Governance: Structure, Management, and Effectiveness", Journal of Public Administration Research and Theory, vol. 18, no. 2, pp. 229-252.

[72] Prahalad, CK and Hamel, G 'The core competence of the corporation', Harv. Bus. Rev., May-June: 79-91, 1990

[73] Russels 2012 Presentation Stanford University 2010 at the EU and US FinES Conference on Emerging Business Models River Publisher 2012 and Russels Martha http://www.youtube.com/watch?v=RrEi-gval78

[74] Sanchez, R 1996a, 'Strategic Product Creation: Managing New Interactions of Technology, Markets and Organizations', European Management Journal Vol 14. No 2, pp 121-138.

[75] Sanchez, R 2000b, 'Product, Process, and Knowledge Architectures in Organizational Competence', Research Working Paper, Oxford University Press, 2000-11.

[76] Sanchez, R 2001c, 'Modularity, Strategic Flexibility, and Knowledge Management', Oxford University Press.

[77] Skarzynski, P. and Gibson, R. (2008) Innovation to the core, Boston, Harvard Business School Publishing.

[78] Taran, Y. e. (2009). THEORY BUILDING - TOWARDS AN UNDERSTANDING OF BUSINESS MODELINNOVATION PROCESSES. Druid-Dime Academy 2009 PhD Conference. Aalborg, Denmark: Centre for Industrial Production.

[79] Teece, D.J. 2010. "Business Models, Business Strategy and Innovation," Long Range Planning (43:2--□3), pp. 172--194.

[80] Tillich, P. (1951). Reason and Revelation: Being and God. University of Chicago Press.

[81] Tillich, P. (1990), Main Works/Hauptwerke bd 2. Writings in the Philosophy of Culture - Kulturphilosophische Schriften Walter de Gruyter, New York.

[82] Timmers, P. (1998) Business models for electronic markets, Journal on Electronic Markets, Vol. 8, No. 2, pp. 3-8.

[83] Venkatraman N., and Henderson, J. C. (1998) Real strategies for virtual organizing, Sloan Management Review, Volume 40, No. 1, pp. 33-48.

[84] Vervest, P et al., 2005, Smart Business Networks Springer ISBN 3-540-22840-3

[85] Von Hippel 2005 Democratizing Innovation MIT Press, 01/04/2005

[86] Zott, C., Amit, R., and Massa, L. 2010. "The Business Model: Theoretical Roots, Recent Developments, and Future Research," IESE Business School University of Navarra, Barcelona.

[87] Zott, C., & Amit, R. 2009. The business model as the engine of network-based strategies. In P. R. Kleindorfer & Y. J Wind (Eds.), The network challenge: 259-275. Upper Saddle River, NJ: Wharton School Publishing.

[88] Zott, C., Amit, R., & Massa, L. (2010). The business model: Theoretical Roots, Recent Developments, and Future Research. University of Navarra: IESE Business School.

[89] Zott, C., & Amit, R. & Massa, L. 2011 The business model: recent developments and future research "Electronic copy available at: http://ssrn.com/abstract=1674384"

[90] Wadsworth, Y (1998) What is participatory action research? Action research international is a refereed on-Action research is published under the aegis of the Institute of Workplace Research, Learning and Development, and Southern Cross University Press source: www.scu.edu.au/schools/gcm/ar/ari/p-ywadsworth98.html.

[91] Walter, A., Ritter T., & Gemünden, H.G. (2001) Value creating in Buyer-seller relationships. Industrial Marketing Management, 30(4), 365 – 377.

[92] Whinston, A.B. Stahl, D.O. and Choi S., The Economics of Electronic Commerce, Macmillan Technical Publishing, Indianapolis, IN, 1997.

[93] Woodruff, R.B., (1997) Customer value: The Next source of competitive advantage. Journal of Academy of Marketing Science, 25(2), 139-153.

[94] Wouters, M.J.F., Anderson, J.C. & Wynstra, J.Y.F. (2005). The adoption of Total Cost of Ownership for Sourcing Decisions Elsevier

[95] Brousseau, E., & Penard, T. 2006. The economics of digital business models: A framework for analyzing the economics of platforms. Review of Network Economics, 6(2): 81-110.

[96] Penrose E. T., The Theory of the Growth of the Firm, John Wiley, New York (1959)

[97] Penrose E. T., The growth of the firm-a case study: the Hercules powder company, The Business History Review 34(1), 1e23 (1960);

[98] X. Lecoq, B. Demil and V. Warnier, Le Business Model, un Outil d'Analyse Strate´gique, L'Expansion

[99] Management Review 123, 50e59 (2006).

[100] Seelos, C., & Mair, J. 2007. Profitable business models and market creation in the context of deep poverty: A strategic view. Academy of Management Perspectives, 21: 49-63.

[101] Teece, D. J. 2010. Business models, business strategy and innovation. Long Range Planning, 43: 172-194.

APPENDIX 1 LIST OF BUSINESSES TESTED WITH THE BM CUBE FRAMEWORK AND THE 7 DIMENSIONS

Primary cases in this paper - Vlastuin, HSJD

Secondary cases for this paper - AH Industries, EV Metalværk A/S, Human Company, Margit, Skive El Service,X-FLEX, GP Rådgivning, Subzidizer, Censec

APPENDIX 2 BUSINESS MODEL COMPONENTS AND DIMENSIONS

Table 5 Business Model Components and Dimensions

Source	Specific dimensions and components	Number	Empirical support Y/N	E-commerce /general /Other	Nature of data
Abell 1980	Customer function, Customer group, customer technology	3	Y	G	N
Porter 1985	Suppliers, Buyers, Competitors, New entrance, Substitutes	5	Y	G	
Porter (1995)	Value Chain activities – primary and support	9	Y	G	
Horowitz (1996)	Price, product, distribution, organizational, characteristics, and technology	5	G	N	
Viscio and Pasternak (1996)	Global Core, Governance, business units, services and linkages	5	G	N	
Timmers (1998)	Product, Service, information flow architecture, business actors and roles, actor benefits, revenue sources and marketing strategy	5	E	Y	Detail Case Studies
Goldmann , Nagel and Price (1998)	Network, competitors,	2	Y	O	
Sanchez (1999)	Product, Process, Technology, Market, Organizations, Knowledge Architecture	6	Y	G	
Markides (1999)	Product innovation, customer relationship, infrastructure management, and financial aspects	4	G	N	
Donath (1999)	Customer understanding, marketing tactics, corporate governance, and intranet/extranet capabilities	5	E	N	

Source	Specific dimensions and components	Number	Empirical support Y/N	E-commerce /general /Other	Nature of data
Chesbrough and Rosenbaum (2000)	Value proposition, target markets, internal value chain structure, cost structure and profit model, value network and competitive strategy	6	G	Y	35 case studies
Gordijn et al. (2001)	Actors, market segments, value offering, value activity, stakeholder network, value interface, value ports and value exchanges	8	E	N	
Linder and Cantrell (2001)	Pricing model, revenue model, channel model, commerce process model, Internet-enabled commerce relationship, organizational form and value proposion	8	G	Y	70 interviews with CEO´s
Hamel (2001)	Core, strategic resources, value network and customer interface	4	G	N	Consulting Clients
Petrovic et al. (2001)	Value model, resource model, production model, customer relations model, capital model, and market model	7	E	N	
Dubosson -Torbay et al. (2001)	Products, customer relationship, infrastructure and network of partners, and finansial aspects,	4	E	Y	Detail Case studies
Afuah and Tucci (2001)	Customer value, scope, price, revenue, connected activities, implementation, capabilities, and sustainability	8	E	N	
Weill and Vitale (2001)	Strategic objective, value proposition, revenue sources, success factors, channels, core competencies, customer segments, and IT infrastructures	8	E	Y	Survey research
Applegate (2001)	Concept, capabilities and value	3	G	N	
Amit and Zott (2001)	Transaction content, transaction structure, and transaction governance	4	E	Y	59
Alt and Zimmerman (2001)	Mission, structure, processes, revenues, legalities, and technology	6	E	N	Literature Synthysis
Rayport and Jaworski (2001)	Value cluster, market space offering, resource system, and financial model	4	E	Y	100 cases

Source	Specific dimensions and components	Number	Empirical support Y/N	E-commerce /general /Other	Nature of data
Betz (2002)	Resources, sales, profits, and capital	4	G	N	
Gartner (2003)	Market offering, competencies, core technology investments and bottom line	4	E	N	Consulting Clients
Von Hippel (2005)	Users and business	2	Y	O	
Vervest (2005)	Network	1	Y	O	
Prahalad & Hammel (2005)	Competences	1	Y	O	
Lecocq, Demil and Warnier (2006)	Resources and Competences, Value proposition, Organizations – internal and external, Revenues, costs, Margins	5	Y	G	Use case study
Brousseau & Penard, (2006)	Consumer, Values - attributes - tangible goods or information services or their combination, alternative (organizational) processes, assembly of functionalities, , capabilities, profit	6		E	Use case study
Seelos & Mair, (2007)	Customers, Resources and capabilities, supply chain, partnerships, profit, important social development Objectives,	6	Y	O	Use case study of BOP market
Chesbrou gh 2008	Value proposition,	6	Y	G	Use case studies
Johnson et all (2008)	Value, Customers, Value chain - operation, Profit	4	N	G	
Masanell, R. C., & Ricart, J. E. (2009)	an objective (real) entity: choices made in every organization with consequences: particular set of choices an organization makes about policies, assets and governance - and their associated consequences - determine 'the logic of the firm, the way it operates and how it creates value for its stakeholders'.	5	Y	G	Case studies

Source	Specific dimensions and components	Number	Empirical support Y/N	E-commerce /general /Other	Nature of data
Lindgren (2010)	Value propositions, Customers/users, Value Chain [Internal], Competences, Networks, Relations, Profit formular	7	Y	G	
Teece (2010)	market segments, benefits (product/service) customer, features/technologies, assembling and delivery, value offering, business's revenue and cost structures, competitive advantage	9		G	
Casadesus -Masanell, Ramon and Joan Enric Ricart (2010)	Value, User, operation, relations - "logic of operation (the way the different components are assembled and relate to one another), and operates in a particular way to create value for its user".	4	Y	G	
Zott, C., Amit, R., and Massa, L. 2010	Value (Value stream, Value propositions, Customer value) activities, Financial aspects (revenue streams, cost structures, revenue model), exchange partners (delivery channels, network of relations, network relations, logistical streams, infrastructure)	14	Y	G	Literature study
Fielt, (2011)	Value, customer, value chain activity, capability, network, profit	6	Y	G	
Taran et all 2011	Value propositions, User and Customers, Value Chain [Internal], Competences, Network, Relations(s), Profit formular	7	Y	G	
Porter 2012	Network, Values, Customers, Supplier		Y	G	
Lindgren and Horn Rasmussen	Value proposition, User and Customer, Value Chain[internal], Competences, Networks, Relations, Value formula	7	Y	E/G/O	46 use cases

Source	Specific dimensions and components	Number	Empirical support Y/N	E-commerce /general /Other	Nature of data
Chesbrough et all 2013	Value Proposition, market segments, value chain and competences, complementary assets, business revenue - cost and profit, competitive strategy	6	Y	G	3 use cases

Source: Specific dimensions and components Number Empirical support Y/N Nature of data

Appendix 3 Monetary and Non Monetary Business values

Please see Neffics D 3.2. www.Neffics.eu

Appendix 4 Strategic value map Blue Ocean

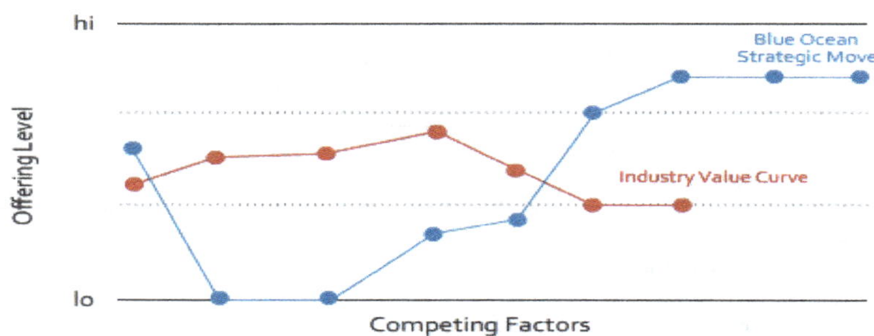

The strategy canvas is the central diagnostic and action framework for building a compelling blue ocean strategy. The horizontal axis captures the range of factors that the industry competes on and invests in, and the vertical axis captures the offering level that buyers receive across all these key competing factors.

Appendix 5 Vlastuin Use Case

Vlastuin is a business started in 1959 and is located in Netherlands. Vlastuin employs around 150 people and had a turnover of 27 million EUR in 2011. During more than 50 years of presence, Vlastuin has added more BMs to its business and thereby slowly

increased its core business. It started off by installing and servicing furnaces and boilers, gradually developed manufacturing and later on added assembling of cranes and parts to the business. A graphical representation of Vlastuin business evolvement can be seen in Figure 8.

Vlastuin's crane business case

The first business case provided by Vlastuin is production of the crane booms. This business started due to the evolvement of the crane producers (Customers) outsourcing crane boom production (Value chain functions). A crane boom is the extendable and retraceable arm of the crane (product) which lifts the loads. See Figure 9.

Vlastuin as a manufacturer of D-Tec container trailers had **competences** of accurate bending and high quality welding (**Production- and process technology** and **HR**) of large heavy pieces of steel, which was exactly what crane producers were looking for. Currently, Vlastuin is a provider of the crane booms (**Value proposition**) to crane manufacturers throughout Europe. The Truck crane BM involves three major stakeholders: Truck crane producers (**Customer**), Crane boom providers (**Network** partner) and Metal sheet suppliers (**Network** Partner). Each of these will be shortly introduced presenting their roles and interconnections between each other.

Truck crane producer business case (OEM customer)

Truck crane producer, as the name implies, produces the cranes and mounts them on the truck. Often they outsource part manufacturing and focus more on final product. Part of the outsourced manufacturing is boom production in which Vlastuin specializes. The truck crane producer has extensive knowledge (Competence) on crane boom manufacturing since it was originally manufactured inhouse. Therefore, they demand same or even higher quality for the outsourced parts (**Value proposition**). Furthermore, in this specific crane boom part provided by Vlastuin, the truck crane producer also has a contract with a metal sheet supplier to ensure that the raw material meets the specifications for manufacturing (**Value proposition**).

Figure 9 An example of a Vlastuin Crane boom on trucks.

Crane boom provider (Vlastuin)

Crane boom provider, or in this case Vlastuin, manufactures (**VC**) crane boom parts based on customer specifications (**VP**). This process starts with the creation of the production drawings and product quality plan (**VP**) by a specialized engineer. Afterwards, special sheet metal is ordered from the supplier (**VC**). After raw materials are received the production processes launches (**VC, C,**). Three major steps in production are laser cutting, sheet bending and certified welding (**VC**). Laser cutting involves cutting out various boom components of the sheet metal plates using laser. This provides high quality cutting edges and very precise component dimensions. Sheet bending is where high dimension heavy components are bent at right angles according to predefined sequences. In order to obtain exact bend angles, very precise laser angle measurements are performed during the process. Certified welding is performed with high-end welding equipment by certified welders (**C**) due to safety regulations of truck cranes. Here, the separate boom components are welded together in a pre-set welding order. This is to avoid crane boom getting twisted due to the heat transfer and thick metal, causing problems later in crane boom operation. After all the production processes are carried out and quality is insured, separate welding assemblies are grouped together and sent to the customer production line (**VC**).

Below, we have summarized the value chain function and process that Vlastuin addresses. It also indicates some of the tangible and intangible value propositions that Vlastuin takes care of together with some of the competences embedded in Vlastuin's BM. Further, it gives an overall view of the **relations** inside the specific BM.

Sheet metal provider

Specifications meeting sheet metal is supplied by a sheet metal provider after the truck crane provider sends out a stock release order assigning certain amount of stock to the crane boom provider. Due to its long manufacturing processes these are manufactured in batches and kept in stock. After receiving an order the sheet metal is transported to the crane boom provider.

For an overall graphical overview of the Vlastuin crane business case, we have drawn up three BMs in action with Vlastuin BM at the center in Figure 10.

One building block is not shown. Our comments regarding the value formula of the crane boom provider Vlastuin is confidential information. In the next case we will, however, be able to go a little deeper into another of Vlastuins BMs.

Business case 2: Vlastuin's paperless manure transportation business case

Vlastuin is also in the manure transportation data administration business. In the Netherlands, it is by law decided that in order to transport manure authorities have to be notified at the start and at the end of the transportation with manure samples. Due to these regulations, Vlastuin started providing AGR units (Dutch for Automatic Data Registration) (**VP**). This unit sends data (VP, **VC, C, R**) to the Vlastuin server where it is filtered and forwarded to the authorities (**Users**). By doing this, it dramatically decreases the processing time and paper work needed for manure transportation (VP) for the user and

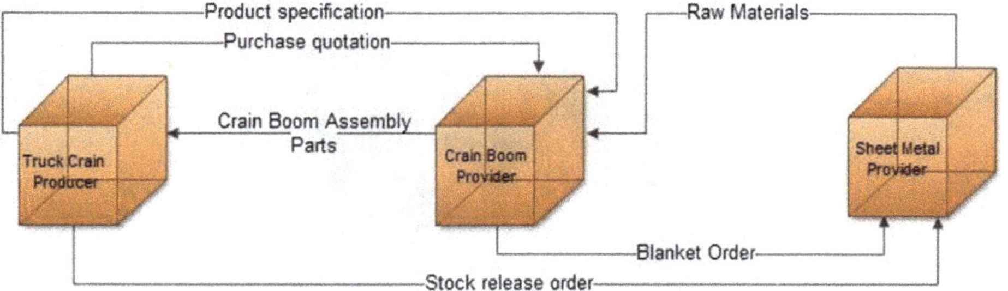

Figure 10 Vlastuin Cranes Business Case Overview.

customers (**CU**). There are eight significant stakeholders in this business case, which will be introduced next.

Manure producer

A manure producer is usually a livestock farmer (**CU´s** customer) who has excessive amount of manure. Farmers usually have a contract with the manure transporter (manure transporter will be explained in more detail later on) (**CU**) which means that all the work that comes with manure transportation is done by the manure transporter. Some examples could be that the manure transporter is responsible for finding manure consumers (**CU´s** customer), or the manure transporter is responsible for all the paper work around the manure transportation (Customers' value proposition demand). The cost associated with manure transportation is deducted from manure producers' payment for manure. The manure producer gets a digital version of the paperwork from the manure transporter.

Manure consumer

The manure consumer (CU´s customer) is usually the farmer who needs the manure as fertilizer for his fields (CU´s customers' (upstream) value proposition requirement). The manure consumer has a contract with the manure transporter which includes all the work associated with manure transportation (CU´s customers' (downstream) value proposition). Manure consumers get the invoice for manure together with the digital copy of the paperwork.

Manure transporter

Manure transporter is the direct customer (CU) of Vlastuin. This usually is the transportation company which transports manure from manure producer to manure consumer. Manure transporter has contract with both manure producer and consumer, and dispatches tank trailers to manure producers upon request. During loading of manure to the tank, samples of the manure are packaged into the sealed bags, as can be seen in Figure 11.

Figure 11 Manure sample bag.

These samples are fitted with barcodes (added value proposition) which are scanned and sent to the authorities together with other required information (**VP, VC, C, R**). This is automatically performed by the AGR — unit via an infrastructure provider service (internal business network partner (**N**) value proposition). After receiving confirmation from the authorities (**N**) about successful transmission, the manure is transported to the manure consumer (**CU´s** customer). The manure consumer is automatically determined by GPS data (added value proposition) combined with manure administration data (added value proposition) thus identifying the closest manure consumer location. Before transportation, the consumer will need to confirm if he wants to receive the manure.

Infrastructure provider

The manure infrastructure provider, in this case the ICT department in Vlastuin (**C**), is providing the platform for data transferring and registration (**VP**). Vlastuin has a server stack which acts as a communication center for manure transportation (**C**). The AGR unit in Figure 12 sends information to the servers with GPS coordinates and scanned sample bag barcodes together with other information (**VC,C,R**). The servers (Network partners (digital) internal Vlastuin) immediately filter out only mandatory information and send this data (value chain functions at internal BM in Vlastuin) to authorities (**CU**). Authorities (**N**) send back a notification to the servers informing if the transaction was successful (external network partners value proposition and value chain functions in BM) where it is forwarded to the AGR unit allowing further processes for manure transportation (VP). In the case where the transaction is not confirmed (which is very infrequent) the problem is addressed manually by calling the authorities and further addressing the problem.

The manure administrator is also connected to the server, which allows access to the laboratory results even though the laboratory (external network partner in the BM) is not connected to the servers directly. All this data can be accessed through the AGR website where the manure transporter provides additional functionalities such as Track-n-Trace (transport movement insights) and consumer specific accounting data. The AGR unit is sold with attached service contact including mobile data connection necessary for communication with the data server together with firmware updates of the unit, and

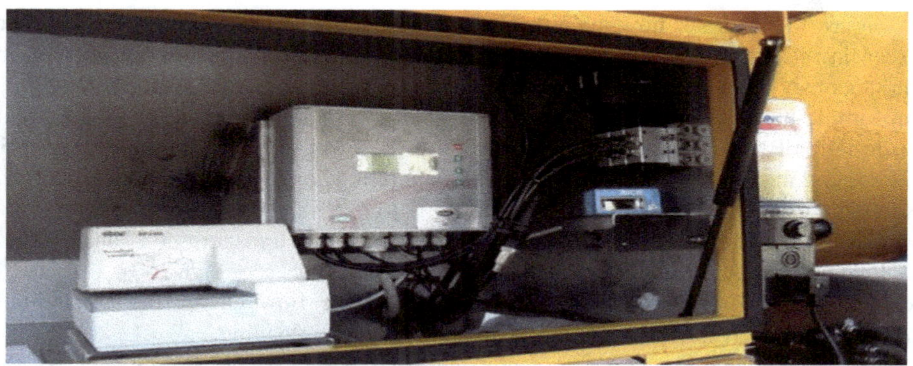

Figure 12 AGR Unit.

software updates for AGR web site. In addition to the AGR unit, Vlastuin also provides D-TEC sampling units which takes the manure samples and packages them to the plastic bags as seen in Figure 11. This unit also comes with a servicing contract together with consumables and spare parts.

Manure Administrator

The Manure Administrator (network partner) provides administrative services (network partners' value proposition and value chain function) to meet the requirements of the fertilizer law. One of the examples could be the application of manure accounting ID from the ministry (value proposition to user demands). The Manure Administrator also feeds data from laboratory results of the manure samples. The Manure Administrator acts as a middle man between authorities and manure transporter, therefore, only the final data is uploaded to the authorities.

Laboratory

The Laboratory (network partner) receives the manure samples for assessment of its value. It identifies the manure producer or receiver by the barcode, and returns their findings to authorities and the Manure Administrator.

Authorities

In this particular case, the authority is the Ministry of Agriculture and Nature management and Fisheries (Users) in Netherlands. They receive the manure transporting data combined with the laboratory results (Combined value proposition).

Regulator

This is the AID (Dutch for General Inspection Service) (User) in the Netherlands. They ensure that all requirements are met by all the participating parties in the manure transporting process. This includes checking farmers, manure transporter infrastructure provider, manure administrator and even the authorities themselves. If any of the requirements are violated, the violating business (or private party) is imposed a fine (**VP** by user).

Figure 13 illustrates how, on a theoretical perspective, at least two "AS IS" BMs can be seen in this particular Manure transportation business case. Vlastuin not only has two simultaneously operational business cases, but looking into manure transportation with just some simple business modeling details shows that the same business case — the Manure transportation Business case has at least two "AS IS" BMs. An overall graphical overview can be found in the following illustrations of manure loading, transportation and unloading business case.

To clarify further the processes in the manure transportation and different stakeholders' process flow chart, readers are advised to see Figure 14, 15 and 16 documentation. In order to more easily understand the flow charts, the transportation processes have been split into loading, transportation and unloading.

As can be seen in this very fragmented and small part of the Vlastuin's business, there are many "AS IS" BMs in operation. It can also be seen that many business partners — network partners — in the overview are shown each with their "AS IS" BMs.

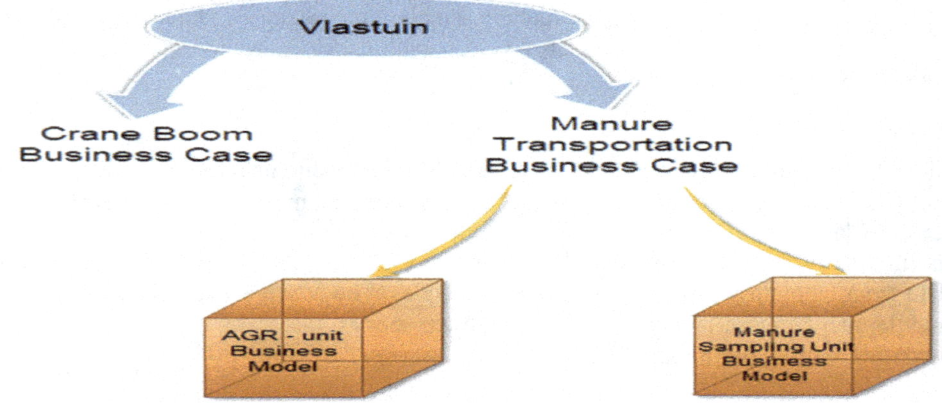

Figure 13 Vlastuin Business Cases and Business Models.

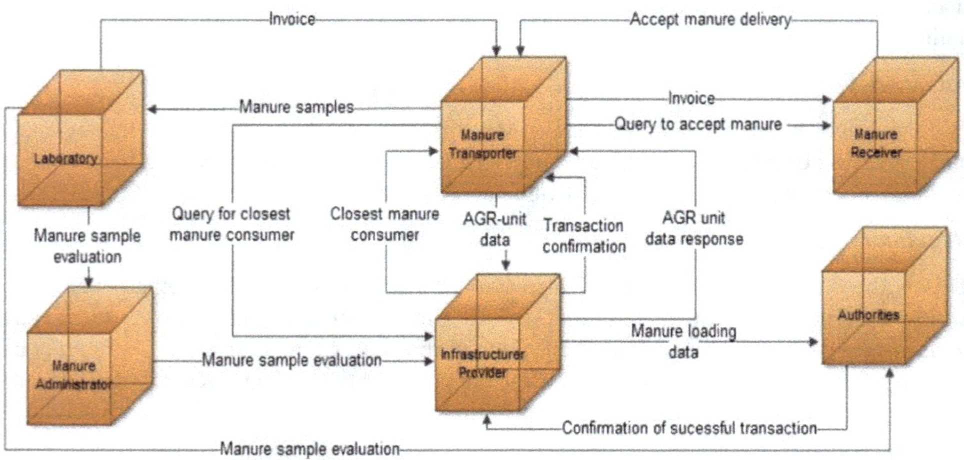

Figure 14 Vlastuin Business Cases and Business Models loading Manure.

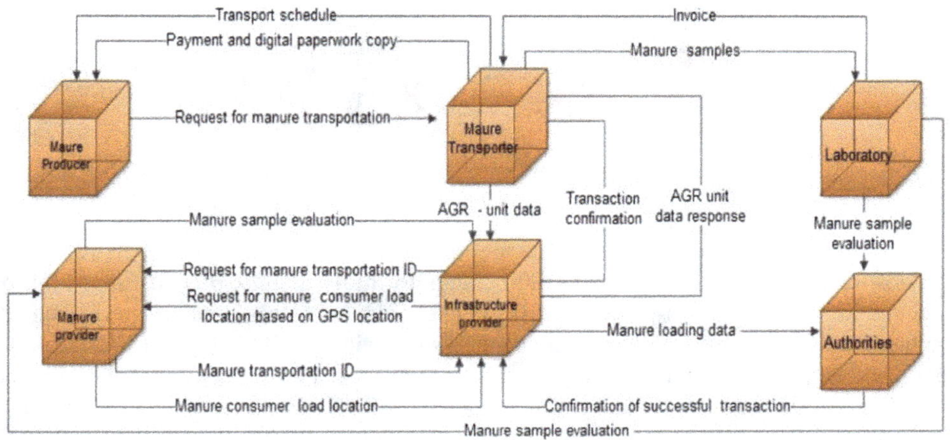

Figure 15 Vlastuin's Business Cases and BMs for Manure Transportation.

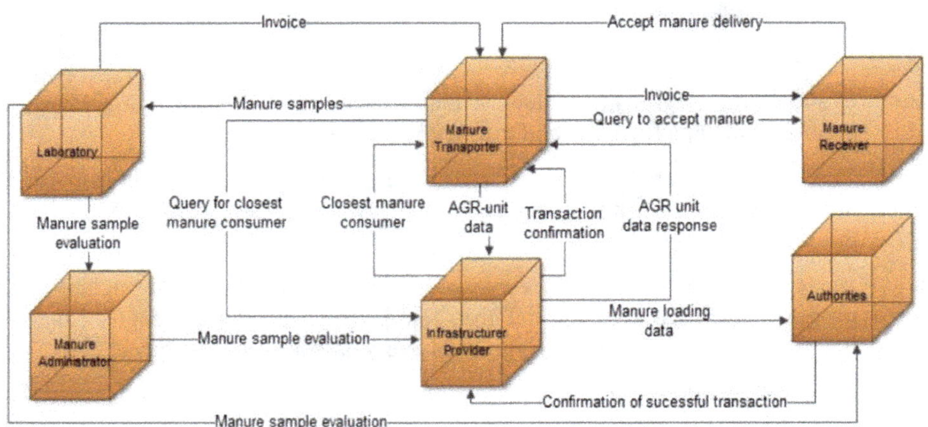

Figure 16 Vlastuin's Business Cases and BMs for unloading Manure.

HSJD Use case

The hospital Sant Joan De Dieu (HSJD) belongs to the Hospital Order of Saint John of God and is a private, non-profit hospital. The order is represented in more than 50 countries and has almost 300 healthcare centers worldwide. HSJD is located in Barcelona, Spain, and is a children and maternity care center. HSJD is a university hospital connected to the University of Barcelona and is also associated with the Hospital Clinic of Barcelona, which helps the hospital to provide top-level technological and human care. HSJD is 95% financed by the Catalonian public system and the remaining 5% comes from private investments. The primary goal of HSJD is to encourage and educate a healthy lifestyle with good nutrition, proper sleep, hygiene and exercise.

The Risk Pregnancy business case

HSJD hospital handles and treats about 4000 pregnancy cases per year. 10% are high risk cases, where the women are in high risk of losing their babies. To postpone the childbirth, the doctor stops these complications and exposes the woman to a daily maternal-fetal monitoring control.

- It is real-time monitoring, concentrated in two parameters:
    - Uterine contraction
    - Fetal heart rate
- It allows the physician to view in real-time the measurement variables of the pregnant lady and her child and to take the necessary measures.
- The realization of this control involves the travel of pregnant women to the hospital, with different frequencies of controls (some have to come every second day, others less frequently)
- It is a contradictory path: since they are high-risk patients, our physicians advise them to not move and stay calm at home. However, the control demands the pregnant women to come to the hospital every day or every two days.

Source: JJ HSJD Hospital

In the "AS IS BM" and in a number of other cases, this control involves patient's admission to the hospital. Today, it is possible to sensor and measure heart rate and other key measurements from the child inside the mother. Those machines and equipment that can measure the child works very well today and nurses can do all the work on preparing and measuring the data from the child.

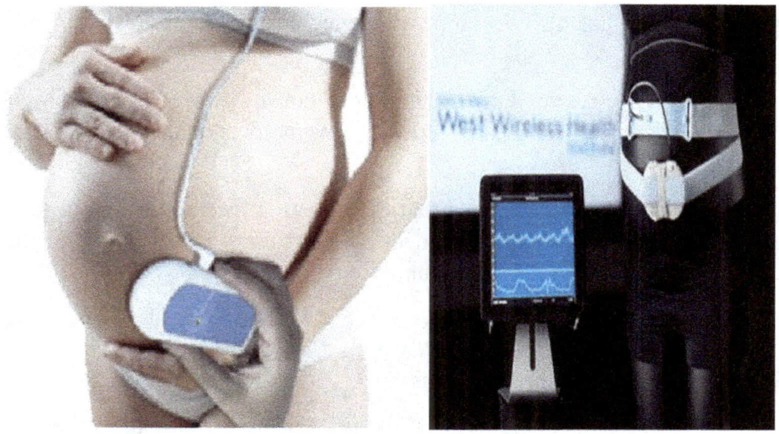

Figure 17 RPU “AS IS” and “TO BE” BM.

Today, the ”AS IS” BM works as the mother leaves her home for a 30 minute visit at the HSJD hospital, where a nurse makes the measurements of the child by putting the equipment on the mother’s “tummy” as seen in figure 17 left side picture.

HSJD´s doctors responsible for the pregnancy “AS IS” BM find it a bit peculiar and not so convenient that they tell the mothers:-

”Don’t do anything — do not move while at home — stay at home”

Source HSJD Doctor responsible for RPU BM

and then they, at the same time, ask them to come to the hospital, transport themselves to the hospital to have the measurements done. Sometimes, the mothers have to come every second day and this is very inconvenient and not a healthy way to act especially for those in risk of losing their child.

The doctors would therefore like to give the mothers another and better solution — as seen in figure 17 right side of picture — something to use at home. They would like to give them some possibility to stay at home and at the same time measure the child. Today it is already possible to monitor diabetes patient in their home.

Doctors and staff at HSJD have worked already two years to find technical solutions and a “TO BE” BM to the challenge and BM ecosystem of risk pregnancy. The result of this work has shown the following challenges seen from HSJD´s perspective

1. Cost challenge — the technique is not cheap enough. Technology has to be affordable to implement. One technology costs 3000 dollars with camera, screen and so on per mother.
2. Price Challenge — HSJD will not and cannot charge the mother
3. Provider and cost challenges — West wireless institute, California US has already developed ”a baby sensor” which costs 25000 US dollar. They are interested, how much exactly they are interested is not known yet.

4. University of Barcelona has also developed a device but this is not tested in real environment
5. The solution has been presented to the medical house with Philips Monitor Careview equipment, however, Philips does not want to take the risk of tele-measuring pregnancy yet.
6. Physician Challenge — it is well known that the measurement can come out with false negative and false positive measurement. Doctors/physicians relying on the new device might then risk falling into some wrong conclusion.
7. HSJD is thinking about how it can involve other physicians outside — near the mother — so the HSJD doctors and experts do not need to be directly involved and HSJD´s "market area" can be increased

When we were initially presented with the "TO BE" Risk Pregnancy BM use case, we were not aware of the multitude of the "TO BE" BM and BMI potential for HSJD. This was carefully studied before making the final choice and decision for one or two "TO BE" BMs. Figure 18 illustrates the map of "AS IS" BMs and the proposed "TO BE" BMs registered in HSJD.

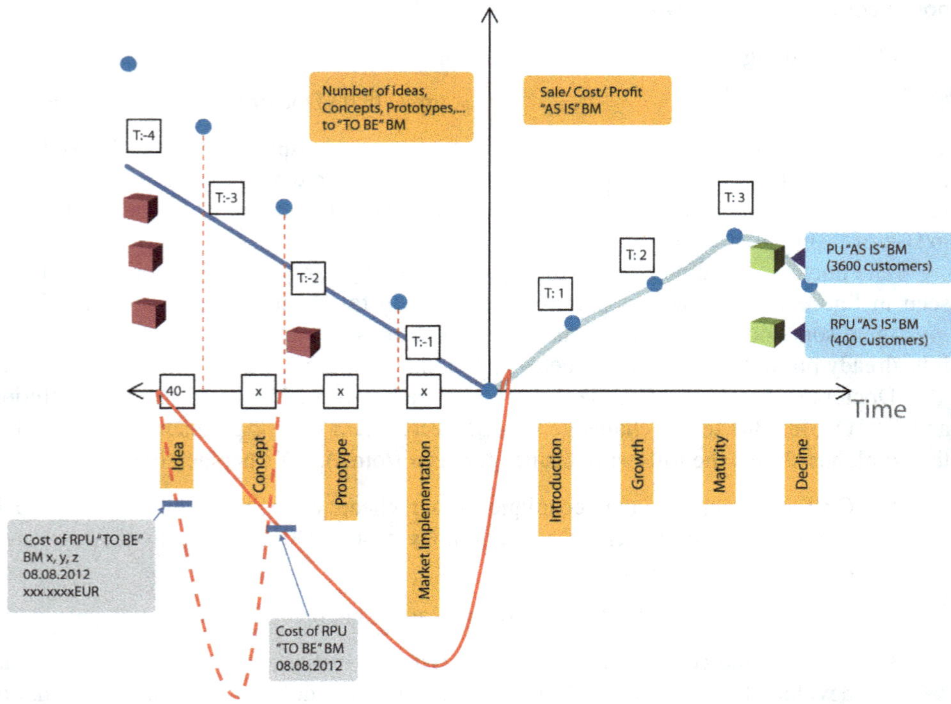

Figure 18 A sketch model of the BMI and BM projects in focus in RPU use case analysis related to BM and BMI lifecycle.

The RPU "TO BE" BM is a new BMI initiative from HSJD's management which involves increasing HSJD´s activities to also doing RPU with support of high technology equipment. Therefore, this initiative involves a whole new platform of **value propositions** from HSJD, new **customers** and **users**, new **value chain functions**, new competences, new network partners, new relations and maybe new value formulae. This could be classified as, to some degree, radical innovation on many of the BM´s dimensions and components. It could also address and increase the BM ecosystem for risk pregnancy as the "TO BE" BM could address markets in Iraq and Morocco.

The RPU center is in the "TO BE BM" and in the first phase it is addressing a well-known user and customer group in Spain, but in future it would consider also addressing new **user and customer** groups external to the hospital, which will to some extent be radical related to previous target groups. However, we classify this change in first phase as incremental related to most BM dimensions, however, HSJD must be aware that the customers' environment is now outside HSJD´s control and the BM is operating outside the HSJD physical business environment together with new network partners (teleoperators, equipment operators) which can be risky.

The **value chain setup and functions** that have to be carried out in the RPU "TO BE" BM are now related to some functions, however, HSJD has great experience in the internal and core functions of handling the functions of RPU Women. The functions outside the HSJD hospital are new to HSJD and some of these are also outsourced to network partners as can be seen below.

HSJD has until now controlled most of the value chain functions around the handling of users, customers and network in the RPU BM. A well-developed handling program has been tested and is operating. Now, the "TO BE" BM involves other network partners. So this is all new to the HSJD pregnancy department — to some extent, a radical BMI. HSJD solved this via outsourcing some of the functions to professional network partners — telecom companies, equipment providers e.g.

Competences also have to be developed for technology, HR, organizational systems and maybe also the culture. This can also mean radical innovation.

Network partners are new — relations are not known especially the external network partners. However, all the relations internal in the BM are known but have to be built up from scratch. Therefore, we also classify the change on the network building block as kind of radical.

The RPU "TO BE" BM value formula is not known yet but it seems as if it may be different to other BMs in HSJD as its point of entry is related to different success criteria and different **value formulae** than profit and other BMs in HSJD.

With these characteristics we would classify the RPU "TO BE" BM as seen in Table 6.

Seen in another diagram, the RPU's "TO BE" BM could be characterized, to some extent, as a risk project as it is changing some building blocks related to the "AS IS" RPU BM in HSJD seen above.

This is very much dependent on which of the several RPU "TO BE" BMs HSJD would choose to implement.

In Figure 19, we propose the space in which the RPU "TO BE" BM can be positioned in terms of its *degree* of innovativeness by means of its radicality, reach and complexity.

Table 6 Classification of Incremental and radical BM innovation related to the 7 dimensions for the RPU "TO BE" BM

Building block	Incremental BM Innovation 'Do what we Do but Better'	Radical BM Innovation 'Do Something Different'
1. Value Proposition	Offering 'more of the same'	Offering something different (at least to the business)
2. Target Users and Customer	Existing market	New Market
3. Value Chain Architecture [Internal]	Exploitation (e.g. internal, lean, continuous improvements)	Exploration (e.g. Open, Flexible, Diversified)
4. Competences	Familiar competences (e.g. Improvement Of Existing Technology, HR, Organizational System, Culture)	Disruptively new, unfamiliar, competences (e.g. New Emerging Technology, New HR Skills, Organizational Systems, Culture)
5. Network Partners	Familiar (fixed) Network	New (Dynamic) Networks (e.g. Alliance, Joint Venture, Community)
6. Relations	Continuous improvements of existing relations (e.g.channels)	New Relations, Relationships (e.g. Channels Physical, Digital, Virtual, Personal)
7. Value Formulae	Existing processes to generate revenues and values followed by/ or incremental processes of retrenchments and cost cutting	New processes to generate revenues followed by /or disruptive processes of retrenchments and cost cutting)

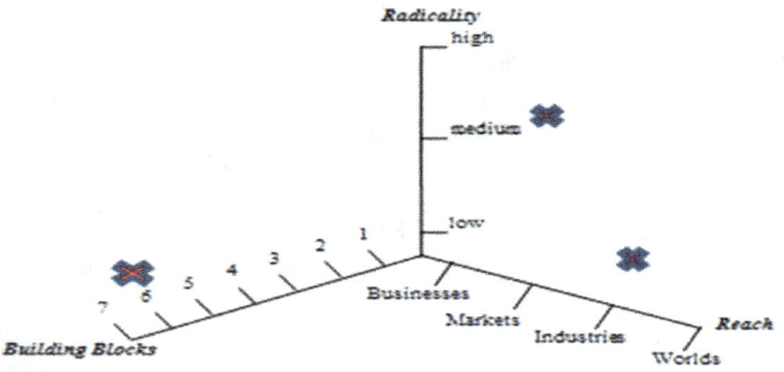

Figure 19 A three-dimensional business model innovation scale – Risk, Complexity and Reach of the RPU "TO BE" BM.

As can be seen, the RPU "TO BE" BM is radical on innovation of building blocks and it is also complex as it is changing six out of seven building blocks. Finally, it can also be classified as far on reach as it is addressing a BM new to the business, market and industry.

As also agreed upon the presentation of the three BMI use cases in detail, the Neffics consortium would be documented within WP 2 D.2.3. Therefore, for further details about the use cases please see WP 2.

APPENDIX 6 BM COMPONENT LIST

Table 7 BM Component list

BM dimension Concept	Group of BM Components	BM Components
Value Proposition	Product, Service, Process of Product and service	Values, Attitudes, Attributes, Tangible and Intangible Values
User and Customer	A person, A Family, A business	Roles
Value Chain functions – [Internal]	Primary functions Support functions	Functions and/or activities necessary to run the BM - inbound logistics, operation, out bound logistics, Marketing and Sales, Service – – Procurement, Human Resource Management, Administration and Financial structure Business Model Innovation
Competences	Technologies HR Organizational System Culture	Product- and service technologies Production technologies Process Technologies Employees and people
Network	Physical Network Digital Network Virtual Network	Roles
Relations	Tangible relations Intangible relations	Relations, Links
Value Formula	Formulae	Formula of price and cost expressed in monetary and/or nonmonetary term.

BIOGRAPHIES

Peter Lindgren is Associate Professor of Innovation and New Business Development at the Center for Industrial Production, Aalborg University, Denmark. He holds B.Sc. in Business Administration, M.Sc. in Foreign Trade and Ph.D. in Network-based High Speed Innovation. He has (co-)authored numerous articles and several books on subjects such as product development in network, electronic product development, new global business development, innovation management and leadership, and high speed innovation. His current research interest is in new global business models, i.e. the typology and generic types of business models and how to innovate them.

Ole Horn Rasmusssen is Post-Doctoral Fellow at the Department of Mechanical and Manufacturing Engineering, Aalborg University, Denmark. He is also a consultant, project leader and researcher at Aalborg University, and a networker at DJØF. He was earlier a supervisor, Ph.D./Researcher/Fundraiser at Aalborg University and a Ph.D./Researcher/Fundraiser/Research fellow at POENOR. Ole Horn Rasmussen has immense experience in the area of structural changes and transformations related to the evolution of organic agriculture.

PERSUASIVE BUSINESS MODELS

Peter Lindgren [1], Morten Karnøe Søndergaard [2], Mark Nelson[3], and B. J. Fogg[3]

[1] *Department of Mechanical and Manufacturing Engineering, Denmark*

[2] *Department of Learning and Philosophy Aalborg University, Denmark*

[3]*Center for Persuasive Technology, Stanford University, California, USA*

Received: 20 February 2013; Accepted: 28 February 2013

Abstract

This paper will look into how persuasive technologies can be applied into business models in specific business models that apply change in social, society and ecological behavior. We look at which of these business models succeed and which do not and address what abilities and triggers we might increase to change not only attitude but also behavior, when applying business models based on positive ecological, social and society behavior. Focusing on a well-established step-wise persuasion innovation process we start out by identifying past experiences with these types of business model and micro-payments introduced to support change in ecological, social and society behavior.

The pivotal question being, how we get people to make a micro-payment when supporting Business Model´s applying positivesocial, society and ecological behavior. Finally we will brush-upon, how the suggested persuasive business models in a business model context, might also be adapted into other business models and lines of behavior with similar feats. In context of the latter, it is suggested, that there is a potential new business model eco-system on the rise in this field. In order to counteract these effects and create leverage the idea of performing a bundle of business models – a multi business model approach - with persuasive technology embedded is introduced.

Keywords: Persuasive business models, Multi business models Business Models and micro-payments, Business Models and social capital, business model eco-system, persuasive technology

Journal of Multi Business Model Innovation and Technology, Vol. 1, 71–100.

1. INTRODUCTION - WHY BUSINESS MODEL INNOVATE?

In the past ten years the number of persuasive technologies in our everyday life, have increased many-fold. The study of these technologies, and how they affect our lives and routines, has become a study of great interest (Fogg 2012). Industry and public players alike are keenly devoting themselves to understanding how different persuasive technologies might be designed, so that desirable behaviors are obtained. Consider, for example, how your GPS kindly warns you not to use while driving. This is good behavior - to you, and your fellow road users. Or think of, how fitness APPs (you surely have one) might help squeeze that little extra effort out of you, not to speak of, how online social networks can generate vast real life changes, ranging from romantic relationships (memories could bring a smile to your lips) to overthrowing corrupt governments (remember the Arab spring). In other words, tremendous impact can be obtained, if the desired message is transmitted, accepted and carried out as a new behavioral pattern. However, getting this right from the beginning is far from easy and forefront business model researchers and practioners in the area are therefore very much devoting themselves to the design question.

In this matter we shall draw on B.J. Fogg's eight step design process to creating persuasive behavior (Fogg, 2009) and relate this to Business Models and Business Model innovation focusing on changing social, society and ecological behavior. Simply listed the eight steps involved in Fogg's model are:

1) choose a simple behavior to target

2) choose a receptive audience

3) find what is preventing the target behavior

4) choose an appropriate technology channel

5) find relevant examples of persuasive technology

6) imitate successful examples

7) test and iterate quickly

8) expand on success.

As, explained by Fogg the eight steps are not intended to be used as a rigid formula, and corners are ment to be cut. For instance, there is very little flexibility concerning the technology channel, as there is already in most cases designed a fixed system to use in the use cases we focused on and studied. On the other hand there is a lot of flexibility concerning target behavior and audience.

Digging into the details, in this paper we will look into how persuasive technologies can be applied to change behavior related to business models. Working with Fogg's approach we accept that climbing Mount Everest is done one step at the time, which means that our challenge is divided into a number of smaller steps. The very first is to study the "simple behavior" the business models target to change. This targeting tie in with the technology at hand, which can be a piece of integrated software allowing people to make micro payments when e.g. pushing a "green" button in our printer console (Karnøe et al, 2012) or a "charity button" in a bottle automat (Charity Button Case appendix 1). This in effect means that when handing in used bottles for recycling we are all able to make micro-payments that will be allocated to saving wild animals, re-foresting or/and other social and society programs, so that the overarching and global social, society and ecological consequences of mans act be leveraged. A piece of integrated technology in a recycling bottle automat, which allow us to make micro-donation that will be allocated to help wellbeing projects in WWF – (www.wwf.dk) and Red Barnet – (www.savethechild.dk). About 1100 bottle automats have this persuasive technology installed in their BM, which make it possible to customers to donate the whole or part of the recycling bottle money by pushing "the charity button".

2. Design/Methodology/Approach

The behavior we will target, is simply, how we make people "push the button"? How can we persuade someone to adopt a certain behavior and "buy" a Business Model? And, when doing so, what will the most perspective persuasive business models look like? And how can we build in the persuasive technology in the business models. To come to grips with this challenge, we will start out by looking at previous successes and failures in relations to business models and micro-payments related to social, society and environmental issues. We will then evaluate, and try to identify the biggest barriers to the target behavior and persuasive business models as such. We will address the issues of ability and hot triggers and then try to identify what the optimum set-up in terms of these persuasive business models would be. The framework of this article is then in the "save the world" category and scale, but our goal is much simpler, as we hope to generate a better understanding of what might persuade people in their everyday life to "push the button" and create environmental, social and/or societal leverage.

3. Business Cases - Examples to Learn From

Addressing the challenge of making people do micro-payments in relations to such business models have been brushed upon before and in this chapter we focus on putting some examples to the front. We will dig into the detail of each case, and try to identify, what worked and what was not successful.

Table 1 Purpose of persuasive business models related to ecological, social and society behavior

Purpose and scopes of persuasive business models
Life aid – helping and supporting people to get out of poverty, illness, clean water
Health care – helping people to better healthcare, fighting diseases, getting medicine
Education – helping and supporting people to education
Investment in things – helping people to clean water equipment, energy- and lighting equipment, community and cultural building and equipment, schools
Business development – helping entrepreneurs or small enterprises to develop business
Environmental protection – Carbon reduction, energy efficiency and renewable energy
Society development – supporting people to re build, build up communities, infrastructure

Persuasive Business Models with Micro payment and Micro financing is carried out in many forms. They are also related to many different purpose and scopes.

The list is properly larger however through our case study we found that some overall groups of persuasive business models exist. Some business models address some very specific areas and are very clear in objectives and structure. Others are more blurred in their focus and give donators more opportunities – but also more difficulties to understand and track to their donators. Some business models projects we therefore had to place in more than one group of persuasive business models. In the following we take out one and in some cases two use case to exemplify each group. For a more detailed use case description this can be seen in appendix 1.

3.1. *Group 1: Life and healthcare issues (Simpa, CBM, TCE, KB, PCBD, RAD, CSA, HSJD, SOS)*

These BM´s have their main focus on life aid due to hunger, war, earthquake, decease e.g. or generally focus at health care as preventing or diminishing AIDS, Cancer e.g. In this group we also placed business models which address more indirectly life and healthcare purpose by preventing people from using unhealthy energy sources.

The objective of these BM´s e.g. the TCE use case, as one representing this group, is to reach total control with AIDS in Southern Africa. TCE builds upon the belief that people by them self can win the battle of AIDS and prevent the HIV infection, while all people can participate via micro donation in "this battle". TCE is micro financed via sales of a special TCE newspaper either by paper or electronically. The overhead of the business models is used for the project

3.2. *Group 2: Projects and things (Schools, buildings, issues (Simpa)*

These BM´s have their main focus on supporting projects, financing things, co-financing projects and things.

Simpa Networks saw that worldwide, approximately 1.6 billion people have no access to electricity and another 1 billion have extremely unreliable access. Without ready access to electricity, the poor depend on kerosene lanterns and battery-powered flashlights for light. Kerosene lanterns are dangerous, dirty, and dim. Worse, they are very expensive to operate. And yet, in most markets, kerosene lanterns are the preferred lighting system. For a person with little or no savings, no access to formal credit, and low and uncertain income, the selection of kerosene lighting is eminently rational. Simpa developed a solar based micro payment light system and business model, where the consumer pays via mobile connection pr. Use of the system.

3.3. *Group 3: Community, social responsibility and society issues (Simpa, CCA, KB, SOS)*

These BM´s have their main focus on supporting initiatives related to community development, personal and social support to people suffering from decease or supporting their relative, helping poor children to education.

The Church Cross Army collects "stuff" that people do not any longer want to keep and then sell these items in special CCA shops. The money collect is then donated for certain social and community projects or send to rural areas for help and support. The products are sold by volunteers and then small money donation from each product is then used for donation. The system has a kind of double donation purpose as people come with their stuff and give it to CCA and then other people can come and buy "the stuff" for a low price. The system further has a recycling impact on society as old "stuff" is reused.

3.4. *Group 4: Environmental and nature – (BA, CBM)*

These BM´s have their focus at environmental issues and protection of nature as e.g. reduction of carbon, water protection, nature protection, protection of places of importance to human beings.

By pushing a "charity button" at the bottle automat (Appendix x) at the largest retail chain in Denmark Coop (www.coop.dk) it is possible to donate bottle recycling money to wellbeing projects in WWF – (www.wwf.dk) and Red Barnet – (www.savethechild.dk). About 1100 bottle automats have this extra button in Denmark. It is possible to donate the whole or part of the recycling bottle money. This is done by pushing "the charity button" first, and when the customer reaches the amount they want to donate then they push the charity button. Afterwards the rest of the bottles and cans are delivered and the pay button is pushed and a cash ticket can then be changed to cash at the cash register.

British Airways' is another example in this group as they decided in 2008 to establish a "unique One Destination Carbon Fund" where they toke customers flight ticket donations and used them to support energy efficiency and renewable energy projects in communities in UK. BA was targeting parts of UK that BA thought needed the most help to improve their economic and social well-being. The funds were managed a not-for-profit charity fund, using the UK Carbon Reporting Framework as quality insurance. The donation funded a range of projects from helping install solar hot water in community swimming pools, small scale wind turbines for schools or energy efficiency measures in social housing.

3.5. *Group 5: Business Development – (IBS, SBT, GB)*

These BM´s have their focus at business development and/or making it possible for people in general, poor people to establish new business or businesses based on social capital and social benefits.

Cell phone banking have revolutionizes financial services for the poor. A woman manages e.g. a village from one cell phone for a project in rural Bangladesh. Another woman manage equally in rural area in South Africa food supply and banking. SKS, Indias biggest microfinance institution (MFI) expects that an infusion of private capital will spur even greater growth in credit to India's rural poor, where nearly estimated 27m of whom are already microfinance clients (MFI 2010). Banks and cell phone companies are taking advantage this expansion of cell phone use in developing economies to extend financial services to roughly 2 billion people, who use cell phones but lack bank accounts.

3.6. *Group 6: Entertainment (Flatr, RAD, CSA)*

These BM´s have a focus on entertainment as driver to sponsoring, donating and micro financing of a business as such, a project or organizations activities.

The latest years there has grown a new world filled with entertainment, news and tools made by everyone, that can support social interaction and community development. Social micropayments projects of this type, that let you support bloggers, developers and other creators and enjoy their contributions to the net, are increasing. Click on buttons to reward great web content or add Flattr to your site is one example of this. Customers to Flatr pick how much they like to spend per month on this activity. Then, whenever they see an e.g. Flattr button on any website, that they like, they click it. When they click the Flickr button they get any types of entertainment – gimmick, small play, joke tailor made to the customer. Flickr then count up all of their clicks at the end of each month and distribute monthly spend between everything they clicked on. Flatr - http://flattr.com/ Big change through small donations

L.O.C.´s famous artists new CD – (http://www.rodekors.dk/kampagner/loc) was sold via the Red Cross website – (www.rodekors.dk) . By bying this the buyer supported Red Cross work. All the profit from the sales was promised to go directly to Red Cros work. The Artist is hereby used as a platform to sponser aid. Red Cross is dependent of the aid the citizen gives and this is a new initative to the organization. L.O.C. claimed he wanted to help people suffering.

3.7. *Group 7: Energy supply and alternative energy supply (Simpa)*

These BM´s have a focus on helping people to energy supply or alternative energy supply. Especially poor people is in focus.

One-line Pitch - Portable solar charging and light through mobile micro-payments for rural African families was introduced to the market by Simpa. Micro payment-control venture formed after 3 years of direct pay-per-use solar energy trials in rural Kenya. 30 combined related-years of mobile-micro payment and rural outreach experience, operating against a proven way to profitably brought affordable power & light to those who could pay with mobile micro-payment.

3.8. *Group 8: Science donation (KB, PCBD)*

These BM´s have a focus on donation for science especially in health care or it could also be science in other areas as e.g. culture, where there is a strong need for financing or too little resources for science.

More and more retailers are making social responsibility a key component of their standard business practices. The sale of " Red" and "pink" merchandise to benefit breast cancer research has become familiar to shoppers in a Pavlovian kind of way: Consumers see the now ubiquitous pink products and their brains immediately associate the branding with the Susan G. Komen for the Cure global breast cancer movement.

Likewise, big-box retailers such as Gap, Apple Computers, and Hallmark make their customers see red. Make that (Red), as in (Product) Red, a movement dedicated to eliminating AIDS in Africa. At Gap, half the profits from sales of Gap (Product) Red merchandise go to the Global Fund to help finance AIDS treatment and prevention programs on that continent

The Danish cancer fond runs a lottery with more than 20.000 winners in the lottery pr. year. Hereof 10 winners will have 1 mill. Dkr. It is not possible yet possible to sell the lots online. Therefore those who want to donate and join the lottery must pay by bank transfer or payment at the local post office. The profit from the lottery goes to 3 main areas: Research, Information and Support to patients and relatives

4. Findings and Discussion

We now turn to our findings and discussion of persuasive business models.

Table 2 Examples of Persuasive Business models "bundle" of value propositions

Combinations	**Businesses**
1. Environment and social community focus	British Airways,
2. Business development and social community focus	SBT, Gramham Bank
3. Entertainment and social community focus	Flatr, Red Cross, Kræftens Bekæmpelse,
4. Donation and a physical product	PBCD, Red Cross, TCE, Simpa
5. Donation and a Service	SOS
6. Donation and tax reduction	Red Cross, SOS, CSA
7. None	IMS

4.1. *Combination of different value propositions*

Instead of focusing just on one value proposition e.g. life, business development and gaming we found that that several of the use cases we studied used a kind of combination BM´s strategy to attract and "persuade" the micropayment. They "bundle" different value propositions and BM´s. We found the following value proposition combinations as shown in Table 2.

Generally we saw that there is not used more than two value proposition combination in these BM´s. However in 2 cases it could be argued that there were to some extend up to 3 value propositions given. (PBCD, RAD). Having more than one value proposition combinations seems to be critical to the success of a persuasive BM because the business models can get blurred and fuzzy in the perception of the customer. However the choice of different donation possibilities can be favorable to persuasive business models because this can increase the involvement of the donator.

4.2. *Profit and non profit*

The micro finance BM studied shows a variety of profit and nonprofit BM projects. We found that 3 BMs were pure profit BM projects, 7 nonprofit and 4 BM projects which made a kind of combination of profit and nonprofit BM,s - a multi business model approach (Lindgren 2012).

Table 3 Purpose of persuasive business models related to ecological, social and society behavior

Categories	Businesses
1. Pure Profit	IBS, GB, Flatr,
2. Non Profit	CSA, KB, SBT, TCE, SOS, CCA,HSJD
3. Combination of profit and non profit	BA, PBCD, RAD, Simpa, CBM

5. SUCCESS OF A PERSUASIVE BUSINESS MODEL

We now turn to the question. How can you tell that a BM project combining micropayment ecological, social and/or society capital purpose is or has been a success? We line up some of the dimensions for evaluation, which could be considered as success criteria to such:

Table 4 Success factors of persuasive business models

Success Factors	**Achieved**	**Medium success**	**Not Achieved**
1. Technical success – the technical system in the BM's works and operates with success	IBS, GB, Flatr, CSA, KB, SBT, TCE, SOS, CCA,HSJD BA, PBCD, RAD, Simpa, CBM		
2. User and customer success of those donating the money – they feel they get value for money they donate and/or spend	IBS, GB, Flatr, CSA, KB, SBT, TCE, SOS, CCA,HSJD PBCD, RAD, Simpa, CBM	BA,	
3. Networkpartner success – all or most network partner fulfill their goals and achieve their business and business model intention.	IBS, GB, Flatr, CSA, KB, SBT, TCE, SOS, CCA,HSJD PBCD, RAD, Simpa, CBM	BA	
4. Short term success – the BM project success fulfill a short term need – generating money or change for a specific purpose quickly – life aid e.g.	IBS, GB, Flatr, CSA, KB, SBT, TCE, SOS, CCA,HSJD BA, PBCD, RAD, Simpa, CBM		
5. Long term success – the BM project runs for a long time – and creates sustainable and ongoing business and BM development, social and community BM projects.	Flatr, CSA, SBT, TCE, SOS, CCA, PBCD, Simpa, CBM	IBS, GB, KB, HSJD RAD	BA
6. Relations success – the project and organization builds up a long term relation to those donating the money. The donators keep on donating the BM	SOS, Simpa	IBS, GB, Flatr, CSA, KB, SBT, TCE, CCA,HSJD PBCD, RAD, CBM	BA,
7. Value success – the BM project generates value as profit to the business	IBS, GB, Flatr, SBT, PBCD, RAD, Simpa,		(Non Profit BM's (TCE, CSA, KB, SOS, CCA,HSJD CBM BA (Combined with a Profit based BM)
8. Value success – the BM project generates value as ecological value – ecological success	Simpa, CBM		IBS, GB, Flatr, CSA, KB, SBT, TCE, SOS, CCA,HSJD BA, PBCD, RAD,
9. Value success – the BM project generates value as Social success	IBS, GB, CSA, KB, SBT, TCE, SOS, CCA,HSJD BA, PBCD, Simpa,RAD, Flatr,CBM		
10. Value success – the BM project generates value as Society success	IBS, GB, CSA, KB, SBT, TCE, SOS, CCA,HSJD BA, PBCD, RAD, Simpa, CBM		Flatr,

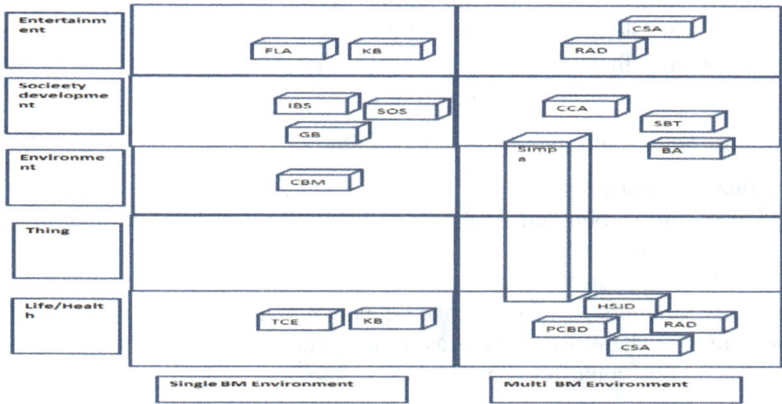

Figure 1 "Persuading tools" related to persuasive Business Models.

As can be seen most of the persuasive business models we studied have been successful in most criteria. – Some have however had minor implementation difficulties in the very early stages. Only very few (BA, GB) and on very few success criteria did not succeed.

It is therefore interesting to have a closer look to how these business models are create, constructed to find out how they achieve their success.

5.1. *How do persuasive BM's get success and how did they change the behavior of people or organizations to donate money?*

The different organizations and projects do their outmost to create and attract micro financing. In this work they try to support or change a behavior in favor of micro payment to a project. They try to relate the micro payment to the above mention list of environmental and social capital issues. They do this both as nonprofit and profit based projects. A cross analysis and summary of the BM projects we studied shows some major difference in scope and objectives as seen in Table 4. As can be seen beneath the persuasive BM´s can be related to different "persuasive tools" which they use to "persuade" donators to donate and change behavior.

As can be seen society, life Health and entertainment are the most used "persuading value proposition". In this context we accept that our case material can be biased as we are primarily studying persuasive business models in social, society and ecological business model ecosystems (Lindgren 2012).

Most of the persuasive business models use a multi business model approach (Lindgren 2012), where they use a combination – bundle - between two or more business models to convince the donators to donate money to their business model. The Simpa and KB business even use more than 3 BM´s.

5.2. *Microfinance and tangible value proposition*

Most persuasive business models seem to come with a kind of **"tangible" value proposition** either **a product**, **a service** or **a process of products and services**. CCA e.g. sells stuff to customers and take the donation out of the profit. RAD use the CD, special coin and signed cd album and Simpa use the solar cell lamp. SOS give the "father" a child which becomes healthcare service, education and the possibility to follow the child and even visit him or her. There is however a big variety in the products and services that is connected to the different micro finance business models. In appendix x we have given an overview of these. Initially there seems to be a strong relations tangible and intangible value propositions inside a BM and between BM´s.

5.3. *Microfinance and intangible value proposition*

Very few micro finance business model use intangible product and services. However BA used this related to saving carbon and supporting community initiatives, but the business model seemed to be a bit fuzzy and unclear both with relation to the saving carbon and to the support fund BM. Further the business model seemed to have difficulties to succeed. It seems as if there was some distance between the donation and the carbon saving together with the funding projects. Therefore it seems as if the donator hereby had some difficulties to relate to the value proposition offered by BA BM.

5.4. *Microfinance and single or multi business model*

Most micro finance BM projects are multi business models, which means that the customer really "buy" a bundle of business models. In BA case e.g. the customers buy a reduction in carbon but also support to a community – and then of course a ticket to a flight travel.

5.5. *Micro finance and technology*

The mobile telephone seems to become more and more important in the setup and operation of BM microfinance projects. Very few of the BM projects were not using the mobile to generate micro financing for their BM´s.

5.6. *Single or Group microfinancing*

Very few of the projects we studied were group funded projects. SBT project was however a group funded project, where the group behind shared the risk of micro financing different social business projects. This means that microfinance project primarily seems to be funded by individuals – "a bottom up approach". However we found some micro finance projects where it was cooperate funded or group funded.

Micro payment and social capital projects is a variety of many individual and few group initiative and investments. Many of the initiatives are carried out by volunteers but others are highly organized and runs as professional businesses. The microfinance business can be focused very short term based aid – focusing at helping people to recover from a catastrophe, hunger – Haiti, Africa. Other initiatives are more long term based – business development, community development, reduction of carbon, reforesting . A lot of these are enabled via micro financing donation in which we give some examples of different type.

5.7. *Micro financing and trust*

We found that persuasive Business models do have to a high degree ti be related to trustfulness. It is therefore vital to the success of the business model that the technology and the organizational structure around the business model are trustful to the donator. If the organizational structure gets too "blurred" the donators will not be attracted. If the relations between more business models gets to complicated then the donator will loose confindence and trust to the business models and not donator to the BM.

5.8. *Micro funding and ownership*

It was also found that it is important that the donator feels a kind of ownership and involvement to the BM´s. This can be established via the BM is strongly matching and related to the values of the donator or the values of the donators business. The persuasive business models must therefore be able to analyze and create a BM which valuepropositions are related to the donators values – otherwise it will be very difficult to achieve success of the business model.

5.9. *Micro financing, network and network construction*

Persuasive business models are often constructed with a rather complicated network physical network (network of people), digital network (ICT network) and virtual network (network that turn up whenever there is a task or a valueproposition that the persuasive business model have to provide. These networks are often very blurred and not ease to the donator to "see". We found that it is therefore very important to those bidding out the persuasive business models to visualize and communicate very precisely how the network is constructed and which network are involved. It seems to be more important these days as the competition and number of persuasive business models increase.

5.10. *Microfunding and nonprofit/profit business model*

As seen in model 1 more persuasive business models use the multi business model approach, where they combinate a profit and a non profit business model. Most business we studied in the persuasive business model ecosystem are nonprofit oriented business. However it is often very difficult to see clearly how these so called nonprofit business really are functioning and if the nonprofit organization is just a smart way of doing business.

5.11. *Microfunding and user-friendliness*

In those cases we studied it was significant that the persuasive business models must be exstremely userfriendly. Especially in the very moment when the donator takes and makes the desion to donate the technology, service and paying process must be very userfriendly, easy and clear.

6. THE OPTIMUM SET-UP IN TERMS OF PERSUASIVE BUSINESS MODELS

Above we addressed some of the issues of ability and hot triggers to persuasive business models and we identify the construction and what characterize a persuasive business model target at changing ecological, social and society behavior.

We now discuss the optimum set-up in terms of these persuasive business models would be.

Our research shows that a persuasive business model at an optimum must adapt a multi business model approach combining different engridience from more than on business model. To illustrate this we use the 7 building block Business model framework (Lindgren 2012) showing two persuasive business model examples.

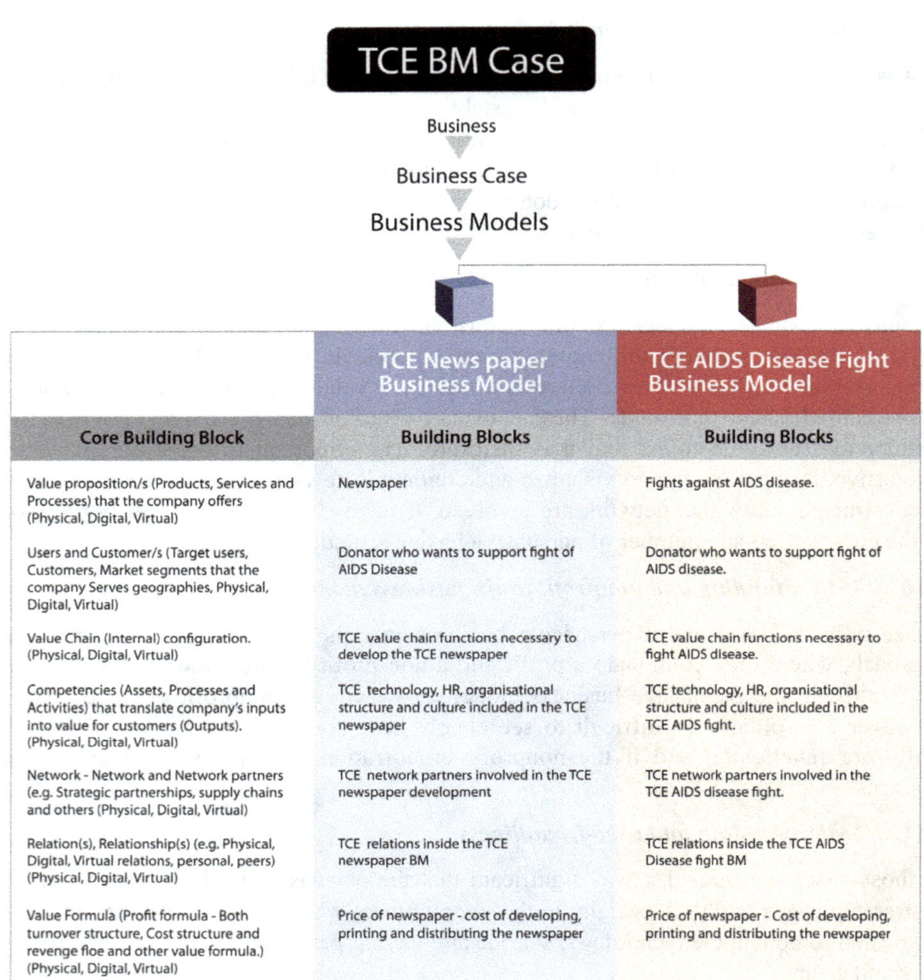

	TCE News paper Business Model	TCE AIDS Disease Fight Business Model
Core Building Block	**Building Blocks**	**Building Blocks**
Value proposition/s (Products, Services and Processes) that the company offers (Physical, Digital, Virtual)	Newspaper	Fights against AIDS disease.
Users and Customer/s (Target users, Customers, Market segments that the company Serves geographies, Physical, Digital, Virtual)	Donator who wants to support fight of AIDS Disease	Donator who wants to support fight of AIDS disease.
Value Chain (Internal) configuration. (Physical, Digital, Virtual)	TCE value chain functions necessary to develop the TCE newspaper	TCE value chain functions necessary to fight AIDS disease.
Competencies (Assets, Processes and Activities) that translate company's inputs into value for customers (Outputs). (Physical, Digital, Virtual)	TCE technology, HR, organisational structure and culture included in the TCE newspaper	TCE technology, HR, organisational structure and culture included in the TCE AIDS fight.
Network - Network and Network partners (e.g. Strategic partnerships, supply chains and others (Physical, Digital, Virtual)	TCE network partners involved in the TCE newspaper development	TCE network partners involved in the TCE AIDS disease fight.
Relation(s), Relationship(s) (e.g. Physical, Digital, Virtual relations, personal, peers) (Physical, Digital, Virtual)	TCE relations inside the TCE newspaper BM	TCE relations inside the TCE AIDS Disease fight BM
Value Formula (Profit formula - Both turnover structure, Cost structure and revenge floe and other value formula.) (Physical, Digital, Virtual)	Price of newspaper - cost of developing, printing and distributing the newspaper	Price of newspaper - Cost of developing, printing and distributing the newspaper

Figure 2 TCE bundle of Business models related to AIDS Disease.

TCE have in this business case chosen to bundle two business models – one with their TCE Newspaper which generate money and is bundle with their second business model – The TCE AIDS Decease fight Business model. The two business models are both offered to the same customer – the donator. In this bundle of business models the donator gets a thing – the news paper – and the promise of TCE fighting the aids disease in one district chosen by TCE. This is how they "persuade" their customers to donate money to their business.

As indicated in the model TCE could have bundle other BM to these two Business Models and TCE have other BM cases in their Business.

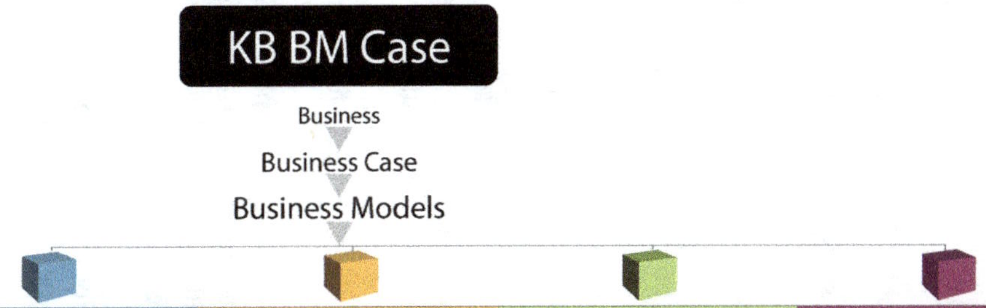

KB BM Case

Business
Business Case
Business Models

	KB Lottery Business Model	KB Cancer Disease Business Model	KB Cancer Information Business Model	KB Cancer Patient Support Business Model
Core Building Block	Building Block	Building Block	Building Block	Building Block
Value proposition/s (Products, Services and Processes) that the company offers (Physical, Digital, Virtual)	Lottery, possibility to win money, things and services	Research aimed at Fighting Cancer disease	Development of Information material aimed discovering and Fighting Cancer disease at an early stage, preventative	Developing and running Cancer Patient Support
Users and Customer/s (Target users, Customers, Market segments that the company Serves geographies, Physical, Digital, Virtual)	Donator who wants to support research in cancer, support of cancer patients, information about cancer	Donator who wants to support fight of Cancer Disease	Donator who wants to support development of information about Cancer Disease	Donator who wants to support development and running Cancer Patient Support
Value Chain (Internal) configuration. (Physical, Digital, Virtual)	KB value chain functions necessary to run the KB lottery	KB value chain functions necessary to handle funding support for cancer research	KB value chain functions necessary to handle information about cancer research, cancer patient support activities, cancer discovery and protection	KB value chain functions necessary to handle Cancer Patient Support
Competencies (Assets, Processes and Activities) that translate company's inputs into value for customers (Outputs). (Physical, Digital, Virtual)	KB technology, HR, organisational structure and culture included in the KB Lottery	KB technology, HR, organisational structure and culture included in the KB cancer research funding handling	KB technology, HR, organisational structure and culture included in the KB cancer information activities and handling	KB technology, HR, organisational structure and culture included in the KB Cancer Patient Support activities and handling
Network - Network and Network partners (e.g. Strategic partnerships, supply chains and others (Physical, Digital, Virtual)	KB network partners involved in the KB lottery	KB network partners involved in the cancer research funding BM	KB network partners involved in the cancer information activities	KB network partners involved in the Cancer Patient Support activities
Relation(s), Relationship(s) (e.g. Physical, Digital, Virtual relations, personal, peers) (Physical, Digital, Virtual)	KB relations inside the KB lottery BM	KB relations inside the KB research funding BM	KB relations inside the KB information	KB relations inside the KB Cancer Patient Support BM
Value Formula (Profit formula - Both turnover structure, Cost structure and revenge floe and other value formula.) (Physical, Digital, Virtual)	Price of lottery - cost of developing and running the KB Lottery	Price of newspaper - cost of developing, running and distributing the KB research cancer funding	BM Price of KB information - cost of developing, running and distributing the KB information BM	BM Price of KB information - cost of developing and running KB Cancer Patient Support BM

Figure 3 KB bundle of Business models related to KB Disease lottery BM, canser research funding , cancer information activity, cancer patient support BM,s .

The KB persuasive business model is much more complicated in its structure than TCE. Firstly it bundles at least 4 business models – the lottery BM, The Cancer funding BM, the Cancer patient support BM and the Cancer Information BM. Although it is said by the KB business that donators like often play the KB lottery knowing that if they do not win then their donated money will be used to something that will be in the could of cancer research, cancer patient support and cancer information then it is much more "blurred" to the donator what his donation specifically go to. KB plays the multi business model approach by bundling more BM´s together and offered this to the donator.

7. Barriers to "jump" to the target behavior and to persuasive business models success as such

How many business models can You play or bundle?. Is there a maximum of business models and a maximum of a bundle of business models. This we have not been able to investigate in our research. However there seems to be a limit on how You bundle business models and how many business model You bundle.

Firstly it seems that persuasive business model bundle with society supporting business models e.g. ecology (Carbon, rainforest protection e.g.), pollution protection, society social issues face harder conditions to success than persuasive business models related to life and health persuasive business models. These persuasive business models could presumably jump barriers to change of behavior or rejection to donation by bundling their business models with other types of business models as entertainment, edutainment, life or health business models.

Secondly it seems that pervasive business models that have smart and easy to operate technology embedded have higher potential for success.

Thirdly it seems that pervasive business models that make the donator personally involved in the donation choice and the donation moment seems to have higher possibilities of success. The personal involvement can either be established via entertainment BM, choice of health care BM (HSJD case – make donator choose between 3 different health care BM´s),

All in all there is several barriers to jump and this is why the BJ Fogg behavior change model can be valuable to change the behavior of people with small steps.

8. "Dark sides" of persuasive business models

Through our analysis of the use cases we also came above some dark sides of persuasive business models

Harnising the social capital in small groups

Persuasive Business models that focus on lending to the poor are e.g. often costly due to high screening, monitoring, and enforcement costs. Group lending advocates that the believe in individuals are able to select creditworthy peers, monitor the use of loan proceeds, and enforce repayment better than an outside lending organization can by harnessing the social capital in small groups. Using data collected from FINCA-Peru (Fiegenberg 2005) exploited the randomness inherent in formation of lending groups to identify the effect of social capital on group lending. She found that having more social capital results in higher repayment and higher savings. She however also found suggestive evidence that in high social capital environments, group members are better able to distinguish between default due to moral hazard and default due to true negative personal shocks.

Leapfrog of traditional banking services and moral

Cell phones have allowed much of the developing world to forgo building an expensive landline infrastructure in rural areas and could now be used to leapfrog traditional banking services. A study by Vodafone suggests that "in a typical developing country, an increase of 10 mobile phones per 100 people will boost GDP growth by 0.6 percentage points." Notwithstanding the potential of mobile banking to expand financial services to the poor, the proliferation of cell phones has had a positive impact on development but also in some cases negative impact. A string of suicides has put micro lending under the spotlight .A messy collision with the realities of local politics made the Indian MFIs think about restriction in microfinancing and micro payment. However MFI finally decided not to and instead focus on talking about something more basic: survival. However politicians from the state of Andhra Pradesh (AP), where microfinance has made the deepest inroads and where SKS has its headquarters – one of the big providers of micro finance- , have held micro lenders responsible for the suicides of 57 people. It was alleged that these people were hounded to their deaths by lenders' coercive recovery practices. MFIs deny wrongdoing. Vikram Akula, SKS's founder, said that although 17 of the 57 women who killed themselves were SKS clients, none was in default so there was "no scope for putting any pressure". Despite this, the state government passed an executive order on October 15th 2005 imposing curbs on MFIs. The order stopped short of capping interest rates, as many had feared, though a subsequent statement by a senior bureaucrat suggested that this remained an option. SKS voluntarily shaved two percentage points off its loan rates in AP, where it had 2.2m borrowers. But it was barely functioning in the state anyway. A series of arrests of so called "field workers" led the business to keep 6,000 staffers idle.

Interest rates too high of persuasive business models

Interest rates of 20-30% may seem high for Micro finance - but so are recovery and loan-servicing costs in remote villages. According to Mary Ellen Iskenderian of the Women's World Banking (Iskenderian 2010), a network of MFIs, a more pressing problem is likely to be over-indebtedness, fuelled by rapid growth in a sector with no formal credit bureaus. This led to that Indian MFIs are now sharing information, pledging not to lend to a person who has already borrowed from three others and to keep total lending to a limit. However smaller lenders have fewer qualms (The Economist 2010)

Persuasive technology to easy to use in Persuasive Business Models

Many persuasive business models have shown to be too easy to use and "too persuasive" leading some donators into serious financial challenges. Above we comment on the easy to lend money via micro loans but also when persuasive business models are related to games and edutainment some donators forget about their economical ability and just "push the button" with out taking their situation into consideration. They are so "persuaded" by the donation situation that the forget about reality.

Persuasive business Models and ethical issues

As more and more persuasive business models move to bundle their business model with edutainment and "life and dead" then they fall into some ethical considerations about the real economical situation and ability of the donator. Still there is no rules to and very few guidelines to these business – how to manage "persuasive business models" in a socieal, society and ethical way.

9. Conclusion

Persuasive BM concept is increasingly gaining acceptance within the business world. The concept of persuasive business models is however not new and especially the church have since long been real experts on persuasive business models – to some extent maybe too clever to run these models..

The concept of persuasive business models has evolved within the increasingly globalized world and environment – however no one have yet defined the persuasive business model. Conversely, the evolution of persuasive business models and new persuasive business models is argued to be just on-going and possibly unstoppable in their process. Thus, this paper has been concerned with the relation between persuasive business models and their road to success we found that one of the main roads to their success is their ability to bundle more BM´s – the multi business model approach. However when the complexity in the bundle of business models increase the persuasive business models face the risk of "blurredness", which can lead to unsuccessful results.

In the study we also looked for - How the suggested persuasive business models in a business model context might be adapted into other business models and lines of behavior with similar feats? In context of the latter, it is suggested, that there is a potential new business model eco-system on the rise and that other business not using persuasive business models could with preference learn from these and even adapt some of their approach to general business modeling.

In order to counteract these effects and create leverage the idea of performing a persuasive business model with persuasive technology was introduced and the significance of the persuasive business models was related to the huge possibilities. On the other hand, the increased competition and the rapidly developing persuasive business model ecosystem have forced businesses and their BMs to become more agile, dynamic and smart in bundling technics. In this context the persuasive business model is highly related to the evolution of ICT, evolution of network based business models , globalization of BM´s and their resources and opportunities availability - hereby involved. However, this raises significant challenges and etical questions in relation to persuasive BM leadership and management.

10. Future Expected Results/Contribution

The study has enlightened a first theoretical attempt to persuasive business models. The next step is to initiate a more thorough and empirical based research to clarify the hypothesis, in order to be able to support and test the persuasive business models on a broader scale.

11. References

[1] Fiegenberg 2005 FINCA-Peru, Figenberg et all (2010) Building Social Capital Through, Microfinance, Faculty Research Working Paper Series, Benjamin Feigenberg, Department of Economics, MIT, Erica M. Field, Department of Economics, Harvard University, Rohini Pande, Harvard Kennedy School, June 2010, RWP10-019

[2] Fogg, B. J. (2009) A Behavior Model for Persuasive Design ACM ISBN 978-1-60558-376-1/09/04

[3] Fogg, B.J. 2012 Persuasive Technology Stanford University Press, Persuasive Technology: Using Computers to Change What We Think and Do (Interactive Technologies)

[4] Economist 2010, January, Micro financing and social capital

[5] Karnøe, M. et al, "A method for collecting fees in a fee-based document output system" 18784US00 (pat. pending)

[6] Lindgren, P. (2012) Towards a Multi Business Model Innovation Model. / Lindgren, Peter; Jørgensen, Rasmus. Journal of Multi Business Model Innovation and Technology 1 edition River Publisher

[7] Neffics 2012 Delivery D 4.3. European FP 7 IOT program – www.Neffics .eu

[8] Iskenderian Mary Ellen of the Women's World Banking, http://www.forbes.com/sites/evapereira/2011/06/16/the-future-of-microfinance-qa-with-womens-world-banking-ceo-mary-ellen-iskenderian/"The Future Of Microfinance: Q&A With Women's World Banking CEO" www.forbes.com/.../the-future-of-microfinance-q..., http://webcache.googleusercontent.com/search?q=cache:Zwde5m0GUt4J:www.forbes.com/sites/evapereira/2011/06/16/the-future-16/06/2011

Appendix 1. Persuasive Business Model Use cases

1. **British Airways' - Unique One Destination Carbon Fund (BA)**

Scope: Environment and social responsibility – non profit, CSR and branding oriented related to BA

Objective: Reduce Carbon, Environmental protection, Social wellfare, social responsibility, community development, nonprofit, branding

British Airways' decided in 2008 to establish a "unique One Destination Carbon Fund" where they toke customers flight ticket donations and used them to support energy efficiency and renewable energy projects in communities in UK. BA was targeting parts of UK that BA thought needed the most help to improve their economic and social well-being. The funds were managed a not-for-profit charity fund, using the UK Carbon Reporting Framework as quality insurance. The donation funded a range of projects from helping install solar hot water in community swimming pools, small scale wind turbines for schools or energy efficiency measures in social housing. BA ensured their customers donation money went to make projects that gave real difference in communities across the UK – via connecting each project to support saving carbon and so its was good for the environment as well as local communities too. BA hereby related carbon saving with social projects in local communities.

Comment: Has not yet in particular been very successful in amount of donation, but to some extend on CO2 and social impact.

2. **Indian, Bangladesh and South African based Micro finance (IBS)**

Scope: Mobile Micro financing business model to poor people at the bottom of the pyramid – profit oriented

Objective: Business development, development of life, profit, new markets

Access to capital and financial services is a problem with in developing countries. Lack of access to banking services hinders economic development and gives the poor no option other than the informal cash economy, leaving them vulnerable to risks and without any means to efficiently save or borrow money. Higher saving rates have proven to make more capital available for investment in development.

> "What we're finding from the evidence from economists is that actually greater access to financial services improves economic growth,"
>
> Jeremy Leach of FinMark Trust, an NGO that promotes financial services for the poor.

> "For many poor South Africans, the system offers a first step into a world that can help them save, send, and receive money. With a few key

> punches, they can send money to a relative or pay for goods without ever seeing a paper bill—a benefit in a country with a high crime rate,"
>
> Source "Nicole Itano of the Christian Science Monitor"

Consultative Group to Assist the Poor (CGPA) estimated in 2008 that 80 percent of people in least developed countries are unbanked. The term unbanked refers to people who do not use simple banking services that the developed world takes for granted, such as checking and savings. Barriers to conventional methods of banking include lack of education, illiteracy, high fees, and proximity to banking facilities.

(Source.: GPFI http://gpfi.org/about-gpfi/partners/consultative-group-assist-poor)

Cell phone banking have revolutionizes financial services for the poor. A woman manages e.g. a village from one cell phone for a project in rural Bangladesh. Another woman manage equally in rural area in South Africa food supply and banking. SKS, Indias biggest microfinance institution (MFI) expects that an infusion of private capital will spur even greater growth in credit to India's rural poor, where nearly estimated 27m of whom are already microfinance clients (MFI 2010). Banks and cell phone companies are taking advantage this expansion of cell phone use in developing economies to extend financial services to roughly 2 billion people, who use cell phones but lack bank accounts. The "dark sides" are comment later.

Comment: Particularly successful in profit term and impact but with some "dark sides"

3. **The Social Business Trust (SBT)**

   Scope: Micro financing business model to develop social businesses – profit oriented

   Objective: Growing and developing social businesses, movement of philanthropy and socially responsibility investment

Social Business Trust ("SBT") is a partnership of six world class businesses, who have come together to combine their resources and expertise to help accelerate the growth of social enterprises. SBT believes there are a number of social enterprises capable of scaling up their operations on a regional and national level and has a clear and ambitious goal: to help transform the impact of social enterprises and thereby improve the lives of up to a million people in the UK. SBT's strengths and capability come from a combination of the partners' commercial and industrial experience; their insights into the needs and sensitivities of social enterprises; and their operational expertise and access to growth capital.

SBT give out "small micro grants" and pro-bono support, with the aim of rapidly growing more than 20 social businesses. The management team behind Bain & Company had initially worked together, supporting social business to scale up. – (http://www.socialbusinesstrust.org/about-us)

Comment: Very succesfull in profit term and impact

Since inception, SBT has made six investments in UK based social business:

Women Like Us [1], The Challenge Network [2], Moneyline [3], London Early Years Foundation [4] Inspiring Futures Foundation [5], Bikeworks

Social Business Trust is part of a wider movement of venture philanthropy and socially responsible investing. SBT was highlighted as a best case study in the 2011 Giving White Paper as an example of how to donate professional and specialist skills.

4. Grameen Bank (GB)

Scope: Mobile micro financing business model - Profit oriented

objective: Fight against poverty,homelessness, destitution and inequality

Microfinance made headlines when Grameen Bank – one of the first microfinance bank - founder Muhammad Yunus won the 2006 Nobel Peace Prize. The cost of the small transactions involved in microfinance— savings accounts, money transfers, and loans to the poor—have been an obstacle. The use of cell phones has verified to cut the cost of such transactions, making widespread microfinance more efficient. A CGAP study funded by the Bill and Melinda Gates Foundation, found that cell phone banking was potentially six times cheaper for routine banking transactions.

"Grameen Bank is a message of hope, a programme for putting homelessness and destitution in a museum so that one day our children will visit it and ask how we could have allowed such a terrible thing to go on for so long", he said. Source.: http://www.grameencreativelab.com/events/worldwide-social-business-day-2012.html

Comment: Very successful both in profit term and in impact.

Muhammad Yunus, winner of the 2006 Nobel Peace Prize and Managing Director of the Grameen Bank since 1985, has been widely recognized as the originator of the use of microcredit as a powerful tool in the fight against poverty and inequality. The Bangladesh-born Fulbright Fellow has a vision of the global eradication of poverty.

5. Flatr (FLA)

Scope: Entertainment micro financing business model

Objective: Entertainment, social capital

The latest years there has grown a new world filled with entertainment, news and tools made by everyone, that can support social interaction and community development. Social micropayments that let you support bloggers, developers and other creators. Click on buttons to reward great web content or add Flattr to your site. Customers to Flatr pick how much they like to spend per month on this activity. Then, whenever they see a e.g. Flattr button on any website, that they like, they click it. When they click the Flickr button they get any types of entertainment – gimmick, small play, joke tailor made to the customer. Flickr then count up all of their clicks at the end of each month and distribute monthly spend between everything they clicked on. Flatr - http://flattr.com/ Big change through small donations

Comment: Successful to some extend on profit and impact.

6. Simpa Networks (Simpa)

Scope: Energy saving business model to poor people – profit oriented

Objective: Energy access to Poor people, safer energy, cheaper energy, healthier energy

Simpa Networks was founded by Paul Needham, InfoTech entrepreneur with two successful exits and a dozen years senior leadership experience, most recently at Microsoft Corp. Jacob Winiecki, recognized thought-leader on energy access and former operational specialist with Arc Finance, with over 5 years experience in microfinance and energy access across India, Sub-Saharan Africa and East Asia, and Michael MacHarg, MBA, former micropayments advisor to Arc Finance and former Acumen Fund consultant with over a decade of experience leading global social enterprises across the spheres of energy, finance and health joined the Simpa Networks. Simpa Networks saw that worldwide, approximately 1.6 billion people have no access to electricity and another 1 billion have extremely unreliable access. Without ready access to electricity, the poor depend on kerosene lanterns and battery-powered flashlights for light. Kerosene lanterns are dangerous, dirty, and dim. Worse, they are very expensive to operate. And yet, in most markets, kerosene lanterns are the preferred lighting system. For a person with little or no savings, no access to formal credit, and low and uncertain income, the selection of kerosene lighting is eminently rational. Kerosene lighting has a low initial purchase price and offers a flexible pattern of expenditures over time. The consumer can choose how often and how bright to burn the lantern, and often chooses to forego light entirely for periods when income is unavailable. The kerosene light – with its high operating costs, its many dangers to health and home, its poor quality light and noxious fumes – has been the best choice available. The poor people can't break the cycle of poverty because they can't take advantage of the myriad productive uses of energy. Access to energy is essential for a family's economic livelihood, health, safety, educational achievement, and quality of life – "It's Expensive to be Poor".

Many individual consumers in many emerging markets are making less than $10/day, with the poorest spending up to 30% of their income on inefficient and expensive means of providing light and accessing electricity. Worldwide, low income consumers spend about $38 Billion per year on kerosene for light, another $10 Billion on cell phone charging. Simpa estimates that there is likely a $100B global opportunity for small scale distributed energy solutions, with no clear market leader.

Modern energy systems that meet these lighting and basic electrification needs are on the market for $200-$400 retail. These systems typically include a solar panel, battery, charge controller, at least 3-4 lighting points, a mobile phone charging port and power for charging or powering small DC devices. These solar home systems have proven to be very desirable to consumers who immediately recognize the health, educational, and income generating benefits. Yet households cannot afford the high upfront cost of a quality solar energy system and thus remain locked into expensive fuel-based lighting and battery charging fees. Over the 10 year useful life of a quality SHS, households will spend $1500-$2000 on kerosene, candles, batteries and phone charging. They are paying more than they need to, because they are poor and because their incomes are low and unpredictable. Underscore this fact: In our launch market, India, as in most developing country markets, the low income consumer can actually afford a small solar home system if only they could pay for such a system over time, in small, irregular, and user-defined increments. That is, if the pricing model matched the pricing model they are already using for kerosene, candles, batteries, and phone charging.

Comment: Very successful both on profit and impact.

One-line Pitch - Portable solar charging and light through mobile micro-payments for rural African families was introduced to the market. Micro payment-control venture formed after 3 years of direct pay-per-use solar energy trials in rural Kenya and 30 combined related-years of mobile-micro payment and rural outreach experience, operating against a proven way to profitably bring affordable power & light to those who can only pay with cash-on-hand.

7. **The charity button machine (CBM)**

Scope: Donation Business Model – non profit

Objective: Saving nature, Environment protection, Social responsibility, nonprofit, branding

By pushing on the charity button at the bottle automat (Appendix x) at the largest retail chain in Denmark Coop (www.coop.dk) it is possible to donate bottle recycling money to wellbeing projects in WWF – (www.wwf.dk) and Red Barnet – (www.savethechild.dk). About 1100 bottle automats have this extra button in Denmark. It is possible to donate the whole or part of the recycling bottle money. This is done by pushing the Wellbeing button first, and when the customer reaches the amount they want to donate then they push the charity button. Afterwards the rest of the bottles and cans are delivered and the pay button is pushed and a cash ticket can then be changed to cash at the cash register.

Comment: Very successful related to donation.

The system was tested in 2007 and from September 2008 it has been up and running in all Coop´s retail shops. The donation to Red Barnet and WWF Verdensnaturfonden was in 2010: 7.980.644 Dkr. And in 2011: 7.722.483 DkR.

8. **The TCE project (TCE)**

Scope: Donation Business Model - nonprofit

Objective: Health care, Social responsibility, community development, nonprofit

TCE was developed as a program by Humana People to People. TCE means Total control of the Epidemic (HIV/AIDS-epidemy). The objective of TCE is to reach total control with AIDS in Southern Africa. TCE builds upon the belief that people by them self can win the battle of AIDS and prevent the HIV infection, while all other people can participate in the battle via small donation. The battle against HIV/AIDS is carried out very systematically. A country is divided up into districts and then subareas. One subarea includes 100.000 people. In every subarea TCE employs 50 locale TCE Field Officers within 3 years. Their task is to free the area for more AIDS spreading. TCE Field Officers walks form person to person and inform about HIV/AIDS, and how people can be tested and protect themselves. The Field Officer develops healthcare programs for ill people, pregnant women and children without parents. Further the Field Officer establish nabour support groups, working groups and collaboration with health care organizations together with personal advice to families.

The scope is to fight HIV and AIDS with the "TCE army", who do not work with weapons, but knowledge, innovation, persistence and sticking together. Money is collected for the program more times every year via small donation. This work is especially done by school pupils and teachers, and by selling the TCE-newspaper.

Comment: Successful to some extend in collecting money for the project. Successful related to the impact.

9. "The Churchs Cross Army" (CCA)

Scope: Donation Business Model - nonprofit

Objective: Social responsibility, community development, religious charity project, branding

The Church Cross Army collects stuff that people do not any longer want to keep and then sell these items in special shops. The money collect is then donated for certain social and community projects or send to rural areas for help and support. The products are sold by voluntiers and then small money donation from each product is then used for donation. The system has a kind of double donation as people come with their stuff and give it to CCA. Then people can come and buy the stuff for a low price. The system also have a kind of recycling impact on society as old stuff is reused.

Comment: Successful on collecting money and impact.

10. Cancer reduction "Kræftens bekæmpelse".: (KB)

Scope: Donation via gaming Business Model – non profit

Objective: Health care – specific cancer, Social responsibility, nonprofit, ...

The Danish cancer fond runs a lottery with more than 20.000 winners in the lottery. Hereof 10 winners will have 1 mill. Dkr. It is not possible yet possible to sell the lots online. Therefore those who want to donate and join the lottery must pay by bank transfer or payment at the local post office. The profit from the lottery goes to 3 main areas: Research, Information and Support to patients and relatives

Comment: Very successful and high impact

The big amount of money that the winners get makes a lot of people dreaming and interest to play/donate a large amount of money. The players get a feelling of a 'win-win situation'. Although they don't win, they are always sure, that cancer patients and their relatives will get advantage out of the lottery. In 2011 the lottery gave a total profit of 58,5 million Dkr.

11. Breast cancer aid – "Pink breast cancer donation (PBCD)

Scope: Donation via product or "at the cash register" donation Business Model – non profit

Objective: Health care – specific cancer, Social responsibility, nonprofit, branding

More and more retailers are making social responsibility a key component of their standard business practices. The sale of " Red" and "pink" merchandise to benefit breast cancer research has become familiar to shoppers in a Pavlovian kind of way: Consumers see the now ubiquitous pink products and their brains immediately associate the branding with the Susan G. Komen for the Cure global breast cancer movement.

Likewise, big-box retailers such as Gap, Apple Computers, and Hallmark make their customers see red. Make that (Red), as in (Product) Red, a movement dedicated to eliminating AIDS in Africa. At Gap, half the profits from sales of Gap (Product) Red merchandise go to the Global Fund to help finance AIDS treatment and prevention programs on that continent.

Unlike pink breast cancer merchandise, (Red) products are not necessarily red. But they are hip, such as the popular girl's white angora- blend hoodie for sale at Gap. The word "ado(red)" is written in pink across the front, with a heart in place of the letter "o."

Pink week where another initiative were the retailers and their employees support the donation initiative. At the cash register before paying for the goods the customer is asked if they would donate some money for the breast cancer initiative.

Embracing Better Business Practices - Gap cites, as its reason for participating in the program, that companies in today's world should go beyond the basics of ethical business practices and embrace responsibility to people and to the planet.

It's just the right thing to do, according to Senior Vice President of Social Responsibility Dan Henkle, "it also unlocks new ways for us to do business better."

Comment: Successful on collecting money and impact.

12. Red Cross.: "Artist donation" (RAD)

Scope: Donation Business Model via an artist cd or concert tickets

Objective: Health care, Life aid, … nonprofit, profit, branding, …

L.O.C.´s famous artists new CD – (http://www.rodekors.dk/kampagner/loc) was sold via the Red Cross website – (www.rodekors.dk) . By bying this the buyer supported Red Cross work. All the profit from the sales were promised to go directly to Red Cros work. The Artist is hereby used as a platform to sponser aid. Red Cross is dependent of the aid the citizen gives and this is a new initative to the organization. L.O.C. claimed he wanted to help people suffering. By buying the album in a digital version each donation will give 30Dkr. To Red Cross. If one buys both album 1 and 2 in a dobbelt album they donate 100 Dkr. and if they buy for 500 Dkr. they get a unik Danish Natial Bank developed Red Cross/L.O.C: coint and a singnated dobbelt albumn. The coin is only produced in 500 pieces and the physical dobbeltalbum is also only published in a limited amount. The cooperation with L.O.C. runs for one month and can be bought via L.O.C.s and Red Cross own webplatforms, in CD retail shops, both physical and digital streaming-service platforms.

13. Concerts – Save Africa. (CSA)

Scope: Donation Business Model via group of artist and concert event + cd

Objective: Health care, Life aid, ...nonprofit, branding, ...

Give a hand to Africa was the title of a popsong from 1985 written by Nanna and made in a studio together with 1980'ties most popular Danish pop- and rock musicians as an aid cd for hungry people in Africa . The inspiration came from Bob Geldorf and Midge Ure from 1984 and the American version We Are the World written by Michael Jackson and Lionel Richie. Nanna won the competition to wright the song as red cross had made a completion amongst pop- and rock song writers, who should have the opportunity to write the song. The song was played at television-transmitted support concerts Rock for Afrika.

Comment: Highly successful on collecting money and impact

14. HSJD – The Spanish Hospital

Scope: Donation Business Model via product sells

Objective: Health care, Life aid, nonprofit, branding, ...

The hospital Hospital Saint Juan de Dieu (HSJD) belongs to the Hospitaller Order of Saint John of God and is a private, non-profit hospital. The order is represented in more than 50 countries and has almost 300 healthcare centers worldwide. HSJD is located in Barcelona, Spain, and is a children and maternity care center. HSJD is a university hospital connected to the University of Barcelona and they are also associated with the Hospital Clinic of Barcelona, which helps the hospital to provide top-level technological and human care. HSJD is 95 % financed by the Catalonian public system and the remaining 5 % comes from private investments. One of HSJD challenges relates to finance, because of the increased cutback in the revenue from the Catalonian public system, since the Spanish economic is under a significant pressure. In regard of that one of HSJD goal is to get a stronger foundation of finance and also be more efficient, which HSJD wants to enable though innovative solution and participate in innovative partnerships and networks – herunder micro payment.

In HSJD Hospital Saint Juan de Dieu – (www.hsjdbcn.org) it is possible to buy at the hospital shop several products with the logo of the hospital. When the customer is asked to pay they are also asked to decide whether the profit of the product should go to one of 3 healthcare project.

1. Help for Children from Somalia to be operated at the hospital in Barcelona Spain,
2. Help to children suffering a certain decease
3. Help to poor children in spain to go to dentist.

Comment: Successful on collecting money and impact

15. SOS - Children fond

Scope: Donation Business Model

Objective: Social responsibility, health care, new hope, education, nonprofit,

Many children that have lost their parents through war, illness, hunger e.g. lives alone in deep poverty without any possibility to get education, food or some chariness. As a socalled SOS-father donators can help a child for only 7 Dkr. Pr. day. Hereby the child will get a new home, family, healthcare and education. The fond promise that only 10 % will be used for administration and no one will be tied up to the agreement forever. This means that the SOS-farther can stop payment at any time. The full amount of money can be used as tax reduction. Further it is possible to follow at a website what the money is used for. Further the SOS-Father will receive a SOS-news magazine.

A. Product, service and process related to micro finance business models.

Project	Product Physical	Product Digital	Product Virtual	Service Physical	Service Digital	Service Virtual	Process of product and service
1.BA (BA)	Ticket	Ticket	CO2 reduction	Community investment			
2.IBS (IBS)	Money	Bank account			Bank service		Money and bank service
3. The Social Business Trust (SBT)	Venture Money for micro Social capital project investment			Board membership and professional help to set up business			Support during the process of setting up and running the business
4.Grameen Bank (GB)	Money	Bank account			Bank service		Money and Bank service
5. Flatr (FLA)	Money to social capital responsible business, products and projects	Flatr logo on the vendors website to click on Track of clicks and accounting			Entertainm ent Track of clicks and accounting		
6. Simpa Networks (Simpa)	Solar cell lamp and source operated by mobile telephone	Mobile lightning Track of use and accounting		Lightning	Track of clicks and accounting		Mobile service and light
7. The charity button machine (CBM)	Get rid of bottles and cans Money back from bottle and cans	Money will be sent to the WWF and Red Cross					

8. The TCE project (TCE)	Newspaper Money send and used by The TCE project			TCE operation – information, workshops e.g. in the TCE areas			TCE process of "fighting the AIDS"
9. "The Churchs cross army" (CCA)	Get rid of old and unwanted stuff			Handling and taking care of the old "stuff" and sending the "profit" to the projects			
10. "Kræftens bekæmpelse" (KB)	Lottery lot If winning Money Promise that the money will be spend according to the aim of the lottery and KB´s statements			Funding service to researchers, support groups and information service activities			
11. "Pink breast cancer donation" (PBCD)	Products if RED action Possibility to donate via the cash register if Pink action. Security that the money will be donated according to the objectives and purpose	Digital donation and Payment service		Taking care of the money handling so that the money falls in to the right hands according to the purpose of the "red" and "the Pink" project			
12. Red Cross.: "Artist donation" (RAD)	CD, Special coin, Special signed Album	Digital ordering and Payment service		Having LC to sign the albums Transfer the money to the right purpose and organization			
13. Concerts – Save Africa. (CSA)	Concert, Concert tickets	Digital ordering and Payment service		Transfer the money to the right purpose and organization			
14. HSJD – The Spanish Hospital	A product in form of a HSJD moscot, a book			Taking care of the money handling so			

(HSJD)	for children, and other products from the HSJD shop			that the money falls in to the right projects of the 3 projects			
15. SOS - Children fond (SOS)	A certificate that the donator is a "Father"	Digital ordering and Payment service Track and trace of the money flow		Taking care of the money handling so that the money is given to the child sponsored			Track and trace of the how it is going with the child sponsored

Biographies

Peter Lindgren is Associate Professor of Innovation and New Business Development at the Center for Industrial Production, Aalborg University, Denmark. He holds B.Sc in Business Administration, M.Sc in Foreign Trade and a Ph.D in Network-based High Speed Innovation. He has (co-)authored numerous articles and several books on subjects such as product development in network, electronic product development, new global business development, innovation management and leadership, and high speed innovation. His current research interest is in new global business models, i.e. the typology and generic types of business models and how to innovate them.

Morten Karnøe is Professor in humanistic knowledge processes and culture-driven innovation at the Department of Learning and Philosophy at Aalborg University, where he also is Director of the Interregional Centre for Knowledge and Educational Studies. His research is primarily focused on technology, innovation and culture. In recent years his major area of research has been culture-driven innovation, facilitating mergers between cultural knowledge and specific innovative areas. He has published widely, both nationally and internationally, on a number of areas such as innovation, technology diffusion and economic development. Furthermore Morten has extensive experience in project management and guidance at both national and international level. From 2008 (initiated 2009) to 2010, Morten build, secured funding for, and took leadership on an EU Interreg IVA project – IKON - incorporating 48 institutional partners, and more than 300 individuals, in Norway, Denmark and Sweden (see: http://www.ikon-eu.org/). Management tasks involved all aspects from accounting over HR to research leadership. Morten has in recent years built partnerships with several international companies. He has been visiting professor at Stanford University in 2011 1nd 2012, and was also in 2011 appointed Aalborg University expert in innovation

Mark Nelson is a senior researcher at the Persuasive Technology and Peace Innovation Labs at Stanford University. Mark Nelson is project lead at EPIC Global Challenge, researcher and practitioner at Stanford University's Persuasive Technology Lab, and founding member of Stanford's Peace Innovation Lab. In addition, Nelson is founder of

Peace Markets and advisor at Gumball Capital. He was previously advisor at Vipani.org and Panango.org and an independent business consultant.

B. J. Fogg is a Professor at Stanford University. Dr. BJ Fogg directs the Persuasive Tech Lab at Stanford University. A psychologist and innovator, he devotes half of his time to industry projects. His work empowers people to think clearly about the psychology of persuasion and then to convert those insights into real-world outcomes. BJ has created a new model of human behavior change, which guides research and design. Drawing on these principles, his students created Facebook Apps that motivated over 16 million user installations in 10 weeks. He is the author of Persuasive Technology: Using Computers to Change What We Think and Do, a book that explains how computers can motivate and influence people. BJ is also the co-editor of Mobile Persuasion, as well as Texting 4 Health. His upcoming book is entitled The Psychology of Facebook. Fortune Magazine selected BJ Fogg as one of the "10 New Gurus You Should Know".

Towards a Multi Business Model Innovation Model

Peter Lindgren, Rasmus Jørgensen

Aalborg University, Centre for industrial Production, Denmark

e-mail: pel@production.aau.dk

Abstract

This paper studies the evolution of business model (BM) innovations related to a multi business model framework. The paper tries to answer the research questions:

- What are the requirements for a multi business model innovation model (BMIM)?
- How should a multi business model innovation model look like?

Different generations of BMIMs are initially studied in the context of laying the baseline for how next generation multi BM Innovation model (BMIM) should look like.

All generations of models are analyzed with the purpose of comparing the characteristics and challenges of previous generations of BMIMs.

On behalf of these results and case analyses, the paper concludes by proposing a framework for a multi BMIM.

Keywords. Multi business model Innovation Model, Business Model, Business Model Innovation

INTRODUCTION

The transition from the booming markets and economic growth of 1950s, to the highly competitive, internet-based and global marketplace of 2011(Wall Street Journal 2011) has completely changed the game of BMI and how BMIMs are constructed, managed and operated.

The demands to BMIMs have through the years increased in the context of effectiveness, efficiency, agility, flexibility, multi participation, handling of mega data and knowledge exchange. These demands are known to be independent of time, place and things (Lindgren 2010). Several businesses have marked the transition during these generations of BMIMs. The transitions started in the 1950s up to 1970s with the generation of industrial research labs such as Bell Labs and Xerox PARC, moving to the mid-1970s to end-1990s where they were replaced by more market focused BMIMs exemplified with companies such as 3M, Toto and IDEO to Toyota's rapid BMIMs and processes, thereby introducing a whole new range of values to customers within "high speed time". During 1980–1990, customers were included directly in the BMI process. Von Hippel (1986) took this process even further by introducing the 'lead user' method in

Journal of Multi Business Model Innovation and Technology, 1–22.

the BMI process in its very early stages. 3M and Hilti AG are good examples of this new BMIM trend and various companies are nowadays applying these new BMI methods.

In the past 60 years, models of business model innovation (Wind 1973), (Cooper1993), (Eppinger 2000), (Tidd 2006),(Chesbrough 2008) have become ever more sophisticated especially with the development of information and communication technology (ICT). By end of the 1990s, initial empirical data was collected by Chesbrough´s research group paying attention towards the need for more open innovations and exploring the potential of opening up the BM boundaries letting knowledge and competences flow in and out from BMs. Later, in early 2000, Chesbrough coined the term 'open innovation' and in 2008, he extended the scope to also include "the open business model innovation concept" (Chesbrough 2005, 2008), which received significant interest.

Through the 2000s, BMI collaborations became more and more a standard for BMIMs, bringing different network partners together and not the least "bringing back" the customer and users into the very core of BMI and as collaborators in BMIM (Bessant 2008). Companies like Zara Inditex, Zappo, Google, Amazon.com, QQ.COM, APPLE, CBS, Facebook, GITHUB and Tata, all showed different approaches to BMIMs with the aim of increasing a higher degree of network collaboration into the BMIM and BMI process.

In our study of literature, we found the following characteristics of generations of BMIMs as shown in Table 1, which is inspired by Rootweels work Rothwell (1994).

Towards a Multi Business Model Innovation Model

A business's ability to innovate and renew its BM through creative processes (Markides 2008) and quickly being able to execute commercialization (Roos 2008, Ballon 2009, Solaimani 2012) became the mantra in the late 2000s. Predictions for 2011 from Silicon Valley USA, Shanghai, Mumbai, Beijing and Sao Paulo (Gabriel 2010, YouNoodle 2011, Wall Street 2011) pointed to BMI and bringing new BMs to the market within just a week even shorter. According to Rebecca Wang, CEO of Younoodle.com, which represents a platform hosting more than 20000 start-up businesses' BMs worldwide, the demands to speed up the time of BMI are pretty much into the same characteristics as was seen back in late 1990 and early 2000 to products and services (Verganti 2000, Lindgren 2002). Life cycles of BM models become more and more diminished as illustrated in Figure 1.

Because of the diminishing life cycle of BMs, the number of proposed ideas to new BMs has naturally gone up. The market of business model innovation has never before been exposed to so many new BMs and the professional BM developers, the so-called "serial BM developers", have increased tremendously (Forbes 2010).

Multi BMI has therefore turned into a kind of new industry with a number of different supporting service providers (Stanford Workshop 2011, Princeton workshop 2012). In a new BM industry, the BMI task is to quickly develop new BMs and prepare them to a level of where they can be sold to others, even though they are only ideas, concepts or just prototypes.

This trend stresses the importance of having the best, smartest, most effective and most efficient multi BMIM. It became very clear in our research that the old BMIMs were suffering to match these new extreme high speed BMI demands. It is, however, not only a challenge of being faster in evolving new BMIs, but is also a matter of controlling speed, preventing risk, being precise, related to the situational context of different BMIs. Do real

Table 1 BM Framework vs. Generations of BMIM

Description of the generations	Advantages and strength	Disadvantages and weakness	Structure of the innovation process
Technology push. (1950s–mid 1960s) The industrial innovation process was generally perceived as a linear progression from scientific discovery, through technological developments in the firms, to the market place, because science is seen as the starting point. BM building blocks: VP, TC, VC, C, N, R, PF	Preferable when unlimited resources to innovation are given and when it is the aim to innovate and develop technological products at a fast pace. Scientists are given maximum freedom to innovate and develop radical new innovations. There is no restriction in the BMIM as such. Preferable when the innovation task and success criteria of the BMI projects are very clear and narrow; related primarily to solving technology challenges and radical technological innovations.	Little attention is paid to the transformation process, or the role of the market place. Scientific freedom is more important than the research and its relevance. No strategic goals in projects, maybe short-term goals at the project level. No direct relationship with general management. Commercial aspects are incorporated late. No project leader is appointed and therefore final responsibility is not clear. Professional project management practices are not applied.	Linear sequential process from department to department starting with scientific discovery.
Market Pull. (mid-1960s–early 1970s) The market role is the source of BMIs and the R&D organization merely has a reactive role. BM building blocks: VP, TC, VC, C, N, R, PF	Preferable when the innovation task is still very simple i.e. incremental BMI very clearly defined with a primary focus on market and consumer direct needs and demands, and not particularly on customers wants. Preferable when companies need to narrow the success criteria to focus on primarily the same purpose and short term success criteria as cost and to some extend performance.	Neglects long-term R&D programs and therefore leads to "incrementalism". Projects are individual units, strategically relationships between these projects and corporate goals were not yet established. It was impossible to serve company goals that superseded the interests of separate internal clients.	Linear sequential process in a project, starting with market need.

Market pull and technology push combined (early 1970s–mid 1980s) BMI is a process that enables interaction between technological capabilities and market needs at each stage. Communication networks link R&D to in-house functions and link the firm to scientific and technological communities as well as to the marketplace. The goal of the portfolio of projects are aligned with the corporate strategy BM building blocks: VP, TC, VC, C, N, R, PF	Preferable when the combination of technologies push and pull the market. With the introduction of feedback loops and communication networks, partners' focus with the aim of changing the value proposition. Thus, failures are reduced and the success levels of the innovations are heightened. Preferable when innovation essentially functions in-house and when the value proposition is not considered most central. Value focus and value innovation are developing towards the customer's wants.	Focuses on product and value chain innovations rather than market and organizational BMIs. Focuses on the creation of innovations rather than their exploitation. Focuses on evolutionary improvement rather than breakthroughs.	Model of an essentially sequential process with feedback loops and interaction with market needs and state of the art technology at each stage.
R&D in alliances. (mid 1980s–early 2000s) Parallel and Integrated R&D. R&D departments are in a network of internal departments and external organizations. R&D management refers to managing research links, networks and external research environments. Because of the number of actors involved, development processes are scheduled in parallel. BM building blocks: VP, TC, VC, C, N, R, PF	Preferable when cyclical routines and networks of partners in the innovation process are incorporated. The model includes feedback paths so that adaptive steering and learning processes can be made more explicit making the innovation system more flexible. Good when lead users are brought into the innovation process before commercialization in order to enhance efficiency and product quality.	Increased networking and integration with internal and external partners increase complexity. The level of corporation and communication is too low and difficult to handle. Inflexibility in the structure of BMI processes.	Coordinated process of BMI in a network of partners. The required coordination is often attained by system integration (with key suppliers and customers) and parallel development (of components or modules of the innovation).

<table>
<tr>
<td>Innovation networks. (early 2000s–present)
Relies increasingly on electronic tools. Operating real time enables increased speed, efficiency and automation across the network of BMI, thereby widening the BMI system. There is a need for controlling the BMI speed which separates the R from the D.
BM building blocks
VP | TC | VC | C | N | R | PF</td>
<td>Includes focus on various long-term benefits, especially the efficiency and real time handling of information across the BMIM system including internal functions, suppliers, customers, and network partners. Enables parallel information processing, one in which electronic information processing and the more traditional informal face-to-face human contact operates in a complementary manner. Electronic tools are employed in the BMIM in order to operate real time and the company network continues to expand. The internet plays an important role in the BMI system by opening up new windows for creativity.
The BMIM adds two new dimensions to the BM – the vertical and the horizontal BM dimension. Focus is still on single BMI and not multi BMI.</td>
<td>Increasing need for knowledge management in order to handle and systematize tacit and explicit knowledge.
Protection of IPR and knowledge comes into focus. A key question is: how can IPR, knowledge and core competences be protected in an open, dynamic, flexible and integrated physical, digital and virtual innovation environment?</td>
<td>Same basic structure as in fourth generation. The BMI process is electronificated and further emphasis is on vertical relationships (strategic alliances, joint ventures, etc.) and with collaborating competitors.</td>
</tr>
</table>

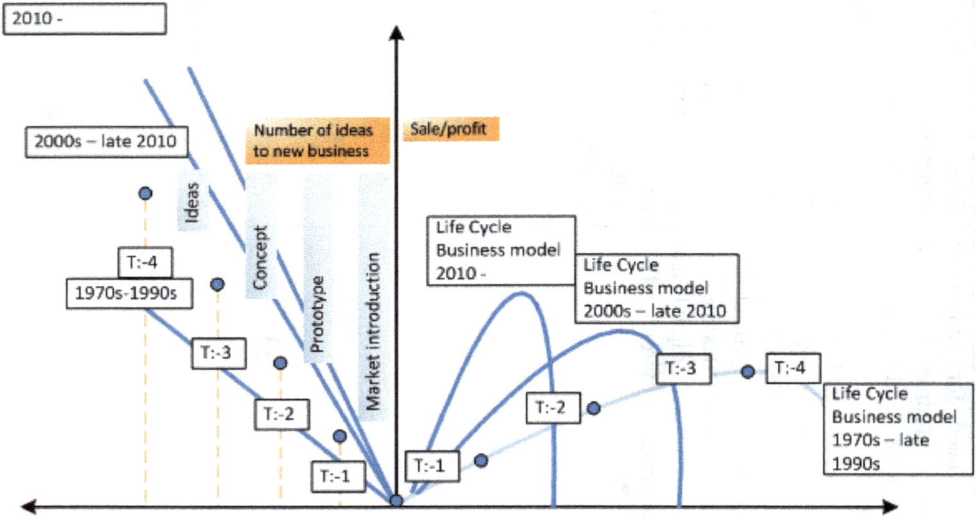

Figure 1 A sketch model of the diminishing Life Cycle and development of BMs (Lindgren, Jørgensen 2010).

time BMI and having different BM from different network partners share values? (Porter 2011).

BMI leaders have, through the different generation of BMIMs, come to realize that competitors relatively easily can and will copy BMs. Today, many examples of quick captures of BMs by global rivals located elsewhere are taking place (Markides 2010), (Wall Street May 2011), (Iphone 5 2012).

In 2010, continuously creating unique BMs through excellent BMIMs was considered to be one of the most important strategic task of businesses to compete with rivals who were quickly copying businesses' new BMs in a market where IPR rights were not respected. (Apple 2012).

In this context, our research on previous BMIMs indicates that there is a strong need for rethinking the BMIM. The BMIM that can support much more complex and knowledge-based BMI with a multi BM approach is preferable. A multi BMIM that can release and pay more attention to intangibles, be more dynamic, be more independent of time, things and place and not least be an integration of physical, digital, virtual and many BMs simultaneously, seems to be the goal. However, the question remains: How would such a model look like?

Design/methodology/approach

The paper is based on literature research on previous generations of BMIMs combined with qualitative case research in four EU and US based BMI cases—Katalabs, Younoodle.com, View World and Peaceinnovation—to assess the requirements and demands to such multi BMIMs. Further, our case findings were presented and discussed at a focus group workshop at Stanford University involving different researchers, consultants, EU representatives and enterprises from seven different countries (Stanford

University workshop 2011) and again in Princeton University 2012 (Princeton University workshop 2012).

This constructs the theoretical and empirical background to propose a framework for the next generation of multi BMIM. The data collection in the analysis has primarily been done through desk research, case research and focussed group sessions with experts and workshops with invited experts in the field of business model innovation. The desk research involved collecting of information through books, articles, and websites. The time frame set for this study goes back from the early 1950s up till 2012. The review mainly covers European and US research within the area.

In the context of literature research, an explorative research framework and design was developed.

A research framework was constructed on the basis of five focus areas:

- The concepts, framework and characteristics of the next generations of BMIMs related to BMI.
- The task of BMI—what will be the most dominated task to be carried out by next generation BMI?
- The field of BMI—What will be the main characteristics of the next generation BMI environment—technology, market, network, competences, relations, where the BM is going to be innovated into and with what?
- The success criteria of the next generation of BMI—What will be the dominated success?
- What is the criteria for BM and BMI tasks?
- The concept of a multi BMI—What will be the main concept/understanding of how to do BMI in the future?
- The Process of BMI is the "way" that the BM follows through the business innovation model from idea to market introduction and so on—How will this process of BMI come to look like?

As earlier mentioned, there has not been any research on the different generations of BMIMs related and compared to the BM framework and context (Osterwalder 2010, Hagmann 2008, Chesbrough 2008, Taran *et al.*, 2008, 2009 and 2010) yet. The aim was, therefore, firstly to establish a comprehensive overview of state of the art knowledge on BMIMs analyzed in connection with BMs and its building blocks. In this context, we first established an overall analytical framework, which can be seen in Table 1.

The structure of the research findings relates the different generation of BMIMs to the BMs and particularly the different building blocks of different generations of BMI models. The analysis is organized so that each generation of BMIM is summarized into a measurement representing:

Green – when the building blocks were very much in focus/represented in this generation of BMIM. The color green symbolizes dominant building block(s),

Yellow – when the building blocks were to some extend in focus/represented in this generation of BMIM. Yellow symbolizes medium represented building block(s),

Red – when the building blocks were in general not in focus/represented in this generation of BMIM. Red symbolizes submissive building block(s).

It has to be stressed that this is not a black and white depiction. If, for example, the competence building block has been proposed to be colored red in a generation, it does not mean that it was not a part of that generation. A business will always have competencies, customers, value chain and so on. Colors merely work as an indicator visualizing that during a particular generation of BMIMs, when seen in a BM context, that those particular building block(s) did not have a central position in that generation and that they were not a main resource to BMI. That is not to say that they did not exist.

The baseline analysis touches upon the BMIM's capabilities related to handling different BMI contexts and thereby lays the ground to our next work and the answer to the question:

What will scenarios of a multi BMIM look like?

In each generation of BMIMs, questions have been asked to better understand and explain the phenomenon and to improve our understanding of the generation of BMIMs related to BMI.

History And Definition Of BMIM

Extensive knowledge exists about innovation models (Wind 1973, Ulrich and Eppinger 2000, Tidd et al. 2009, Chesbrough 2005) and, in particular, on how to innovate products and services (Wind 1973, Cooper 1993, Baker and Hart 2007). There is also a magnitude of theoretical definition of innovation models. In our research, we have adopted this definition: a BMIM is "a business operational manifestation of the way business model innovation works and is carried out" from ideation to market introduction. We have found it to be the most comprehensive one in providing concrete details of a BMIM existing within a business. Consequently, according to this definition, a BMIM serves as a model or a picture that represents the "roadmap" for any BMI carried out in the business. However, these pictures can be very different from one enterprise to another and even within the same enterprise on different innovation tasks.

Consequently, we found that BMIMs can take very different characters e.g. a linear stage gate (Wind 1973, Cooper 2005) or a more flexible, agile and open character (Corso 2002, Coldman and Price 2005, Chesbrough 2005, 2008). BMI models, even if they are certified, may not always be strictly followed (Lindgren 2002). Therefore, one could register a formal BMIM, which the enterprise wants to or says they follow and an informal BMIM which is more in line with what goes on or even supports the formal BMIM to move faster e.g. by "jumping" stage and gates. Further, the "picture" of the BMIM at a given time might—the start up of a given BMI—be totally different to the "picture" followed and seen in a retro perspective context. This may also be true in companies that are ruled strictly by ISO Standards.

There is, however, a lack of knowledge about how and if BMIMs fit into a specific BM context. As we regard BMI as "the tree of innovation" (Taran *et al.* 2010), it is possible for us to analyze the different generations of innovation models in the light of the BMIM context.

The study of the evolution of generations of BMIMs and analyzing them in the BMI context showed that it is not confined to a single discipline. Theories and concepts had to be modified as a result of doing our research and search for the next generation of BMIM. Hence, we adopted an analytical induction method for data analysis (Znaniecki, 1934) in order to improve existing BMIMs and, if necessary, develop new concepts, ideas or subcategories of these.

Berkhout (2006), Tidd (2006), Tidd and Bessant (2009), Hobday (2005), and Libecap, Berkhout, Duin, Hartmann, & Ortt (2007) all rely on Rothwell (1994) research on the evolution on innovation models. Rothwell (1994) has provided a very useful historical perspective on innovation models. He argues that the nature of the innovation models has evolved from simple linear models (1950s-60s) to increasingly complex interactive models (1990s). Rothwell (1994) divides the evolution of innovation models into five generations.

The precepts aspired to in this paper agree with Rothwell (1994) to the extent that there exist generations of innovation models. Regarding the timeframe of each generation, we believe that it is a fluent transition that did not happen from one day to another, but extended for years and for that reason no specific year was the turning point. We have discussed the different precepts and supported them with our own experience and in retrospect analyzed several articles and events showing different changes in society, business and theory and came to the conclusion that the timeframe of the fourth generation stretches from mid 1980s to a period between late 1990s and early 2000s while the fifth generation starts somewhere in late 1990s and early 2000s and onward.

Before examining each individual generation of innovation models, it is useful to emphasize five caveats stressed by Rothwell (1994) in his introduction to the generations: (Hobday, 2005)

(1) The evolution from one generation to another does not imply any automatic substitution of one model for another; many models exist side-by-side and, in some cases, elements of one model are mixed with elements of another at any particular time;
(2) Each model is always a highly simplified representation of a complex process that will rarely exist in a pure form;
(3) Often the progress from one generation to another reflects shifts in dominant perception of what constitutes best practice, rather than actual progress;
(4) The most appropriate model will vary from sector to sector, and between different categories of innovation (e.g. radical or incremental);
(5) The processes that occur within firms are to an extent contingent on exogenous factors such as the pace of technological change.

As we consider BMI as the tree of innovation, we relate different generations of innovation models to BMIM.

CASE STUDY – CONTOUR AND COMPONENTS OF A MULTI BMIM

During 2008 to 2012, we studied several cases. Five of these cases, which we believe represent some of the contours, components and requirements of a next generation BMIM, are presented here.

The Katalabs case

Katalabs is a US based startup company formed out of the same computer science research environment as Google came from, together with the environment around Humanity Lab at Stanford University. In the line of creating a world of WebGL 3D information and communication technology, Katalabs was established. In the Katalabs case, a variety of six BMI projects were studied—BMs that existed before market introduction and BMs that were already introduced to the market. We found a distinction between users, customers and other stakeholders where the users did not pay for the company's products, service and processes, customers paid for the companies' value proposition and other stakeholders paid for the actual or potential value proposition. Because the product, service or process was not yet introduced to the market, BMI was always carried out at a concept, prototype and digitalization level. This was done in a 2D and 3D browser-based BMI environment called Kataspace – www.katalabs.com. Practically all physical elements could be digitalized and brought into this open cloud-based world. Everything that had already been digitalized could be transformed to 2D or 3D objects in the Kataspace environment and all BMI could be carried out and registered 24/7.

The Younoodle.com case

Younoodle.com also comes out of the research and student entrepreneur environment around Stanford University, US. Younoodle created a whole new BMI ecosystem where knowledge entrepreneurs and their BMs could live and where interested stakeholders such as venture capitalists, other companies looking for technologies, other entrepreneurs e.g. could come and join, buy and participate in innovations of businesses and BMs. The BMIM was hereby moved from a single BM perspective to a BMIM that could handle over 20.000 different entrepreneurs business and related BMs in a BM eco system. The continuously increasing numbers of the new BM were self registering information and communication in Younoodles platform, which thereby automatically formed the "DNA" of the businesses, BM, BMI processes and BMIMs. The BM ecosystem visualized, near to realtime, the individual performance of BM ideas and concepts to interested stakeholders.

The View World case

View world is a Private, Public and NGO Partnership business formed around BMI focused at the bottom of the pyramid markets. The BMIM and process is network based and a big number of stakeholders are participating at different levels and times in the BMI process. Stakeholders have very different BMs and the motivation of participating challenges the BMI collaboration environment and model to enable and support this to be possible.

GitHub.com

Github.com is a US business hosting open source and open software code, where companies from all over the world can share software development and share development projects. Any business can join, take and use software from the GitHub open platform. Further development of software is transparent so that anybody at anytime from anywhere can see and follow different lines of the software development (The fork theory 2010).

The Peace innovation case

The peace Innovation case comes out of the research environment at Stanford University. The BMI project in this case was to create a new global BM ecosystem for different BMs related to peace. A BM ecosystem where knowledge-based BM and entrepreneurs based both on profit and highly commercialized BM would work together with semi and non profit BMs. The BMIMs were required to handle many types of BM characteristics, a multi BM approach (Lindgren 2010), with very different BM outputs. Peace innovation had involvements of banks, big global ICT companies, insurance companies, social network companies together with SMEs, volunteers, scientists, all with very different domain backgrounds and demographic placements. Stakeholders were representing interests of BMs with and without profit output as success criteria. The peace innovation

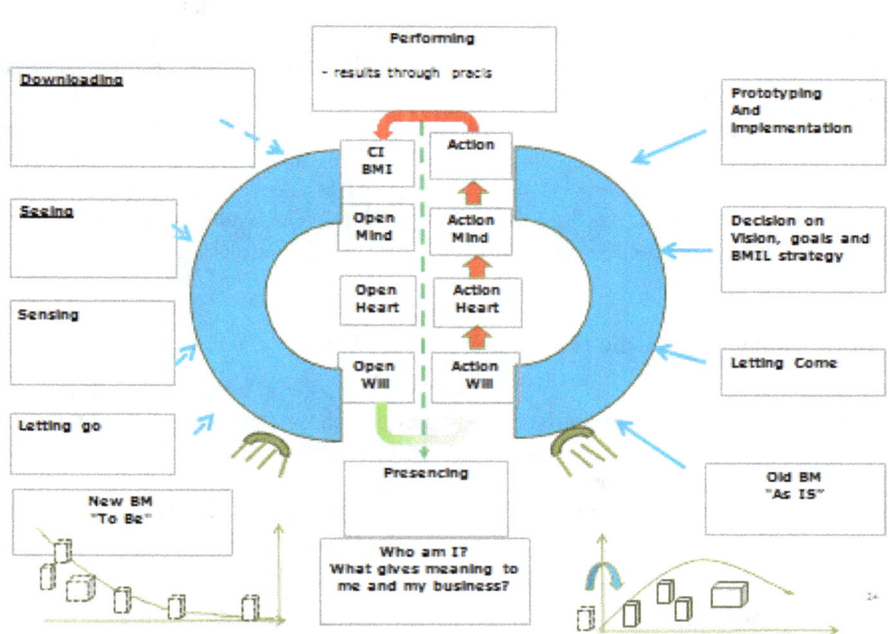

Figure 2 BMI and process related to BMI focus on Old and New BM´s.

case was based on high level field informatics technology, real time BMI with very high and direct involvement of many takeholders. The peace innovation case BMIM wass required to handle the whole chain of stakeholders and their value propositions—a kind of cradle to cradle BMI perspective.

The BMIM and technology developed in the peace innovation project was capable of handling more BMIMs, technology platforms, information and communication technology and interest.

Findings

The next generation innovation model is characterized by fundamentally disrupting previous BMIMs and requiring the ability to integrate and interconnect many different types of BMs, stakeholders' BMIMs and technologies in a distributed network-based BM innovation mode and process.

A full scale implementation of realtime-based BMI, supported by integrated and interconnected BMI technology is and will always be the standard. This enables fulfillment of different stakeholders' demands and requirements of value proposition related to the BMI. Further, it enables and supports handling and bridging of a multitude of BMI technology platform (Nasa 2011) with a strong emphasis on user friendliness and easiness to connect.

BMIM´s are practically a full implementation of the vertical and horizontal knowledge relationship between business, BM and BMI projects and with the highest degree of collaboration between stakeholders involved in the BMI model and process.

The change to a new generation of BMIM will therefore be radical. (Katalabs, Younoodle, Github, View World and Peace innovation).

Synergy and spinoff of the above mentioned is the transition from focus on a single BM to a multi BM approach seen in a BMI ecosystem and a platform perspective of BMIM´s. Beneath a sketch of one of these loops of a BMI process is proposed, which in some sense can be carried out in just few minutes, in real time with continuous iteration and different simultaneously process of BMI (GitHub, Peace Innovation).

A BMI process inspired by the case studies and the U-theory Scharmers 2010.

As can be seen in Figure 2 , the BMI process considers both new and old BMs simultaneously in the BMI perspective. The creativity phase (left side of the model) and the implementation phase (right hand side) is carried out extremely fast and done simultaneously (Github, Peaceinnovation, Younoodle)

The BMIMs will be operating in the physical, digital and virtual worlds based on a multitude of BMs which are simultaneously incremental and radically related to changes in the BMs as seen in figure 3.

A Multi BMI process and context inspired by the case studies Lindgren 2012.

These are continuously in a value adding innovation process, integrated, interconnected and delivered to different stakeholders in a continuous process, wherever and whenever stakeholders demands. The BMIM will be a part of different BM ecosystem and the BMI ecosystems will be part of the multi BMIM, different to previous generation of BMIMs that was primarily part of one or very few BM ecosystems.

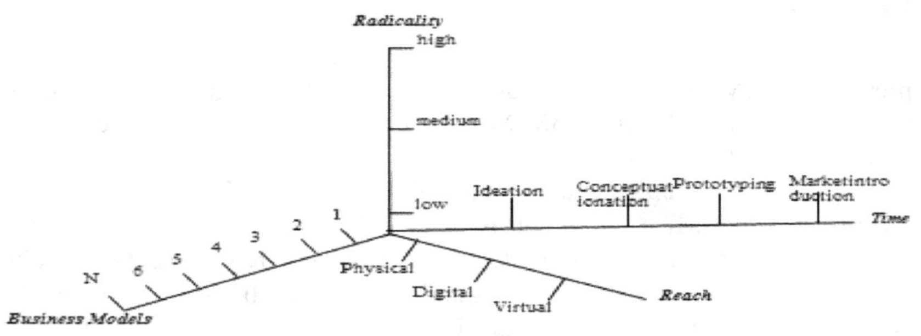

Figure 3 The Business Model Innovation space and process

Not only does the individual BM changes and is brought into a process perspective continuously, we also find that the business is challenged and questioning the identity of the business as such, as BMI now touch on all building blocks of all BMs. This changes the BM in the BM innovation processes, both across building blocks, across BMs, businesses – creating, capturing, delivering and consuming new BM and business constructions continuously.

The multi BM concept (lindgren 2010) seems to be the reality now and in next generation BMIM. It will automatically give BMIM strategic BMI challenges but also strategic potentials. The new advantages and trends in BMIMs with a full digitalization in 2D and 3D real time tremendously challenge the BMIM in relation to the demands for increasing speed, effectiveness, efficiency and automation. It also challenges management overview of what is really strategically going on related to BMI. The business innovation model with the best performance and service tools on these dimensions will, of course, be the winners of BMIMs and BMIM ecosystems. Hereby, we indicate that there will not only be one model.

Transparency in capacity, security, trust and ownership will be central elements in the next generation BMIM. When BMI is brought into the 'clouds'—"Iclouds" (Apple 2011), (Neffics 2012), it enables businesses to release their intangibles of BM building blocks and businesses. This challenges security, risk, IPR and protection of core competences (Lindgren 2010, Walstreet 2011). The strategic dilemma and choice of how to maximize freedom to BMI together with maximizing security when opening up all the BMs including competencies, core competencies and core business to the entire world, becomes of utmost importance and strategic concern to a BMIM. The BMIM that can secure stakeholders on these issues will be the market leader..

Businesses have begun to realize the importance of implementing and innovating their BMs to not just focus on securing competitive advantage and profit. A whole new variety of value outputs of BM is expected. This was documented and stressed upon at our focus group workshop at Standford University on Emerging BMs and BMIMs in May 2011 (Stanford Workshop May 2011). Our existing BM and BMIM understanding seems to be too simple today (Github, Peace Innovation). BMI in the new generation of BMIM completely changes the game and understanding of the BMI, BMIM construction and business understanding. The discussion on the term 'business', which has gained increasing awareness both in literature as wells as in organizations lately (Amidon 2010, Amit et.al 2010, Zott 2011, Fines 2011, WSIE 2012) is real and the question if the business is the right identity to future generation BMIM is important to ask.

Cases and our focus group workshop confirmed that we are in a time of disruptive change, where businesses are actively implementing Open BM and Open BMI because they are free, quick, realtime-based and contribute to a leaner multi BMI process and reduce or even take away direct costs (Katalabs, Peace Innovation). The big question is: How do we handle this strategically in a multi BMI and multi BMIM context?

Start up businesses build their BMs on Open BMs and Open BMIs. Large businesses also follow this trend. This mega trend will change the whole context of BMIs and how BMIMs are created. Openness, visibility, transparency, sharing and speed of BMIMs will take BMI into a new dimension and new era.

Github.com and YouNoodle.com are businesses specializing in handling such open source and open BMI platform and share most of their "open source code" or "open BMs". They are two examples of new businesses which came out of the sky just within 2 years,

Table 2 Next Generations BMIM characteristics

Characteristics of next generation BMIM	
	Realtime-based BMI
	Direct BMI, direct BMI interaction with all stakeholders often on Beta versions of BM
	High degree of BMI flexibility, agility
	Real time BMI and responsiveness
	Stakeholders involved at forefront of BMI project through the whole BMI process
	Vertical and horizontal BMI collaboration and BMI knowledge sharing
	Continuously digitalization of information and communication – use of wikitech technology
	Realtime digitalized documentation and processing of BMI and BMIM
	Digitalized BMI knowledge and learning embedded in all building blocks of every single BM
	Multi BMI
	Strategic BMI overview in 2D and 3D of the multi BMI process
	2D and 3D visualization of tangibles and intangible values, knowledge, stakeholders, value chain, competences, profit formula, processes
	BM and BMIM system are interconnected and integrated in BMI eco systems
	Vertical and horizontal BMI collaboration
	Parallel and integrated BMI process
	Open BMIM with maximum flexibility and agility:
	Facilities and tools for strategic BMI leadership and management at all levels and possible view points
	Fully developed BM and BMI digitalization of everything, everybody, everywhere
	Open access to BMI data and BMI information
	BMI metrics, computer-based heuristics, BMI learning systems
	2D and 3D assisted BMI simulation

becoming important players in new markets of "social coding", "social innovation" and network-based BMI.

Until now, Open BMs and Open BMIMs have not been considered stable enough for established enterprises to practice, but as more businesses are expected to turn to these models,the Open BMIM approach becomes closer to be realized in the next generation of BMIM.

The increasing openness and complexity in BMI encouraged BMIM to involve and attract more stakeholders. This marks a new and disruptive understanding of BMI. Outputs from BM can now be something else than just close customers and traditional stakeholder value fulfillment. Outputs can now also be other values and also seen in a society and sustainability perspective (Peace Innovation, View World and YouNoodle Case), (Princeton 2012), (E-challenges 2012) having an increasing focus on society and networks values of BMs and BMI projects, changing the innovation task to a higher complexity level but on the other side also more and more willingness to try BMs that are early beta types.

This leads to a new criteria and demand for success to multi BMIM, where the early criteria of short-term based focus on cost and long-term success based on improvement and performance are changed to focus on short-term time and long-term learning success criteria with the sustainable value proposition in focus.

These days, businesses such as Google, Facebook and Apple with their ITunes and Iphone apps are experiencing rapid BMI growth and have shown remarkable skills in controlling BMI speed and fitting their BMs to shorter and shorter BMI cycles. At the same time, they are facing increasing demands from individuals, groups and society to meet the values of the society (EU/Facebook 2012).

Table 2 sums up and presents some of the characteristics we found in our research of the next generation BMIM.

The digitalization of the BMIM results in radical change and radical openings of the business. BM **value proposition(s)** offer additional value propositions to more stakeholders in integrated and interconnected physical, digital and virtual world/market. Target stakeholder will play an active role in the BMI enableing innovation of new BM values. The "cloud" creates BM opportunities that before were unthinkable.

The network, relationship and competence building blocks in the BM become even more important players and play an even bigger role in the BMIM and the BMIM processes (Verna Alee, Amidon and Gonzales 2011 at Stanford workshop, Princeton workshop 2012, WSIE 2012, E-challenges 2012). This is because network, relationship and competencies of different kinds and with different connections related to various different BMs and practices are deeply involved, interconnected and of larger importance to realize and commercialize a BM value proposition. Yet, independent of each BMI projects, we found in our case that there is a tendency of a change in value proposition focus to a more process value proposition focus (Normann and Verganti 2012), value network and value relationship focus. This is a disruptive change from previous values and BM output focus regarded as standalone values to values as value relations, shared values (Porter 2011) and value relation networks. A first strong tendency to more focus on values related to society and not to single businesses is therefore our expectation on behalf of our findings (also confirmed by Fines roadmap 2011, 2012).

The complexity of defining business's **target users and customers** hereby becomes significantly difficult and blurred to someone watching from outside a BM innovated from the sixth generation BMIM. Enterprises will change their focus and consider chain of stakeholders and stakeholders' life cycles, vertical and horizontal stakeholders, communities, and stakeholders, even network of stakeholders with different demands for value proposition. The target stakeholders are broader and now include digital and virtual stakeholders which also include machines, hosts, value chains and even the cloud. A rethinking of the term customer, target customer and market segments is necessary.

A BM platform, "an ecosystem for multi BMs", where different BMs can be attached to transfer their value proposition to different stakeholders and other BMs will be standard feature in next generation BMIs. A "BM ecosystem" in a BM platform similar to the ones introduced by Apples Apps system, Git Hub, Katalabs, YouNoodle and Peace Innovation will be standard of BMI. All are nice examples of different BMI platforms, where the producers of apps, open software, digitalized objects, BMs, peace objects cater to "the BM platform", similar to the furniture industry in old days when big chains of furniture producers such as IKEA, Sears, Metro catered to the global demands. Innovating for an ecosystem for BMs is, however, far more complex than innovating for a single BM. It challenges existing BMIMs as it has to cover more BMs at a time, support BMI on a system level and has to match different stakeholder expectations of quality. Apple have tried to solve this by a strict quality assurance system.

Target stakeholders will be given central roles in the BMI ecosystem where the quality assurance process will be enhanced by the advancement of the "cloud". A unique possibility to narrow down who the essential target stakeholders are, a close to 360° view of stakeholders and a much more closer understanding of what values the individual stakeholder gives, processes and supplies before, under and after the buying process.

The digitalization of the BMIM system and the evolution of the cloud into the BM world provide new challenges for the internal **value chain** in enterprises. The internal value chain is an integrated part of the cloud and is open. This increases the complexity of defining the value chain as previously carried out (Porter 2005). The virtual value chain and BM will be standard and part of other virtual value chains and other BMs who only exist when there is a task for them (Coldmann and Price 2004, Vervest et al 2005).

Production of virtual goods, virtual services and virtual processes forces the value chain in businesses into new dimensions of BMI with the aim to serve physical market, digital markets and virtual market places simultaneously. The integrated physical, digital and virtual value chain will be the reality in the sixth generation model.

The view on competencies has to be rethought and changed from being focused on having **competencies** that are inhouse based, to a new understanding where the enterprise's competencies runs its business and related BMs as a part and together with other stakeholders competencies in a field of BMs which we call the network-based BM.

Outsourcing and sourcing were the big mantras in earlier generations of BMI models where new businesses evolved as born globally and born virtually, which set a new standard of competence in innovations in BMI and BMIMs. The necessity for being a fast BM innovator and have fast BMIMs eventually becomes somewhat equal to BMI success and survival in "BM ecosystems". Therefore, this trend will increase even more.

The extended use of virtual value chain leads to a continuous expansion of **networks** involving different stakeholders. Network partners include physical, digital and virtual and increase complexity and the need for focus on knowledge zones and innovation but also to knowledge relationship management—The Innovation Super Highway (Amidon 2008, 2010) .

Finding and leveraging competencies from the right network partners is the critical task in the next generation BMIMs where knowledge in technology, market, network and competences is embedded in enterprise's BM.

Relations will play a key role in the next generation BMIMs as internal and external BM relationship complexity increases and the need for finding, relating and maintaining relationships in new ways with stakeholders are needed to fulfill competence gaps or other functions for the focal enterprise. Relations with many other building blocks in the BM are physical, digital and virtual, which makes communication across BMs possible and visible both in 2D and 3 D.

Relations plays a crucial role in the internationalization of a BM, where different entry barriers on new markets can be passed via relations

The integration with digital and virtual marketplace creates new possibilities for enterprise's **profit formula.** BMs will be accessible 24/7 serving stakeholders demand worldwide. Stakeholders will be attracted by increased numbers and new varieties of value formula continuously.

Multi BMI will include both users who do not pay for products, services and processes, but contribute to BMI with other values and help to develop critical mass so that other customers and other customer groups together with other BMs become possible, achievable and profitable.

It can be argued that the next generation of BMIM would be the first generation of a complete BMI framework, releasing the real potentials of BM´s building blocks. It will still be a challenge to take all seven building blocks of the BM framework into consideration simultaneously and treat them with equally intense effort. Not just that, it will also have to take all the BMs in the enterprises' business portfolio into consideration to remain parallel, integrated and interconnected.

CONCLUSION

The paper commences with an overview of earlier generations of BMIMs where it is possible to see the explanation of why the different generations of BMIMs have changed significantly from one generation to another.

Organizational structures behind the BMIMs changed over the generations from functional structures to matrix structures and further on to network structures. However, with each generation, various disadvantages followed a new generation, which tried to overcome these, but inevitably led to new challenges or disadvantages.

The first generation of BMIMs handled the BMI from department to department and was challenged and had to move into a multi-disciplinary BM project process. This became a standard for the **second generation** and later generations.

BMI projects organized in direct relationship with a business strategy were a characteristic of **the third generation**. The transition to **the fourth generation** involved increased focus on external and internal partners which in a network-organized BMI context created new challenges.

The combination of the first and second generations' technology with push and pull BMIM´s led to the notion that market and technological aspects were considered to be most important throughout the whole innovation process.

In this context, feedback loops were introduced in the BMI processes to prevent faults and bad BMIs. The need for re-evaluation of previous steps during the BMI process was raised concurrently with the increasing complex and multi-phase BMI processes. ,Furthermore, the focus on BMI activities were organized more in parallel to increase speed of development.

The challenges in managing BMIM processes, as can be read above, changed throughout the years from being focused on science, to market, then to customer and finally to a combination of integrated focus and in **the fifth generation** commencing with focus around networks.

It is possible to see that some issues have stood their ground and others have arisen such as the need for competent employees, extensive knowledge about technology and market trends. This view is more cumulative and evolution-oriented in contrast to the static description of the first generations of BMIM´s.

As more dynamic, complex, realtime presentation of the BMI are adapted from the increasing digitalization and internet-based BMI, all five generations of BMIMs require reformulation, remodeling in response to the field of BMI and demand for strategic high speed BMI.

The next generation BMIMs introduce a first generation of a new area of BMIMs. When practicing BMI in 2012 and further on, it would be important to have a BMIM that is excellent and fits with the completely new context of multi global BMI. The agenda of BMI has changed dramatically in the last years, which stress the necessity of a new generation of BMIM. Flexibility, dynamics, speed, independence of time, things, BM, people and place are the characteristics of the next generation BMIMs. Another issue will be that the multi BMI will be performed simultaneously. Through the literature study and case research, we found the contour of the next generation BMIM. Our findings show that some but not all of the challenges and implications of previous BMIM is met by the next generation BMIM.

Further Research

The research calls for further work on the sixth generation BMIM. In our research, we are continuing to investigate the sixth generation BMIMs in several cases in the US, EU, India, Africa and China.

References

[1] Abell, D.F. (1980), Defining the Business: The Starting Point of Strategic Planning, Prentice-Hall.

[2] Amit, R. and C. Zott (2001), Value creation in e-business, Strategic Management Journal, Vol. 22, Nos. 6-7, pp. 493-520.

[3] Apple 2012, http://www.businessweek.com/news/2012-10-01/apple-s-iphone-5-infringes-patents-samsung-says-in-suit

[4] Baker M. and S. Hart (2007), Product Strategy and Management, Harlow: Prentice Hall, pp 157-196.

[5] Ballon, P The platformisation of the European mobile industry, Comunications & Strategies, Dossier: Changeover in the mobile ecosystem, no. 75, 3rd Quarter 2009, pp. 15-33.

[6] Chesbrough, H. and R.S. Rosenbloom (2002), The role of the business model in capturing value from innovation: Evidence from XEROX Corporation's technology spinoff companies', Industrial and Corporate Change, Volume 11, Number 3, pp. 529-555.

[7] Chesbrough, H. (2005) Open Innovation

[8] Chesbrough, Henry (2006), Open BMs: How to Thrive in the New Innovation Landscape, Boston: Harvard Business School Press.

[9] Chesbrough, H. (2008), Open Business Models: How to Thrive in the New Innovation Landscape, Boston: Harvard Business School Press.

[10] Christensen, CM, 1997, 'The Innovators Dilemma', Harper Business ISBN 0-06-662069-4

[11] Cooper, R, 1993 'Winning at New Products' Addison-Wesley Publishing Company ISBN 0-201-56381-91993..

[12] Cooper. R., 2004 Product leadership

[13] E-challenges 2012, Lisabon http://www.echallenges.org/e2012/ - Workshop on Business Values and Business Model Innovation in the networked enterprises of People & things.

[14] EU/Facebook 2012 http://mashable.com/2011/11/28/facebook-european-commission-privacy-advertisers/

[15] Fines Future Internet Enterprise Systems (FInES) Cluster Research Roadmap Version 2.0 15 February 2010

[16] Forbes 2010

[17] Goldman, Nagel & Price, 1998, 'Agile Competitors and Virtual Organisations', Van Nostrand Reinhold, New York.

[18] Johnson M.W., Christensen, M.C. and Kagermann, H. (2008) Reinventing your business model, Harvard Business Review, vol. 86 No. 12, pp. 50-59

[19] Iphone 5, 2012 http://mashable.com/2012/09/12/iphone-5-compared/

[20] Linder, J. and Cantrell, S. (2000) Changing business models: surveying the landscape, Cambridge: Accenture Institute for Strategic Change.

[21] Lindgren, P 2003, Network Based High Speed Product Innovation Center of Industrial production - Buch´s Grafiske ISBN 87-91200-15-6

[22] Lindgren, P, Bohn, K, & Sørensen, B 2004, 'Network Based Product development Leadership and Management – The Impact on Short and Longterm Continuous Innovation', CINet, Sydney

[23] Lindgren, P and Clemmensen 2009 Green Communication The enabler to multiple business models 12th International Symposium on Wireless Personal Multimedia Communications (WPMC 2009)(VITAE) September 7–10, 2009 in Hotel Metropolitan Sendai, Sendai, Japan

[24] Lindgren, P and Kristin Falck Saghaug and Suberia Clemmensen 2009 "The pitfalls of the blue ocean strategy canvas - the importance of value related to the strategy canvas". CInet Brisbane 2009

[25] Lindgren, P and Saughaug 2010 The pitfalls of the Blue Ocean strategy Implications of "The Six Paths framework" CInet Zürich 2010

[26] Lindgren, Jørgensen and Taran 2010 Research on behalf of research on BM introduction and BM lifecycle since 1970 – working paper.

[27] Lindgren and Taran 2010 "A futuristic outlook on emerging Business models" Springer Publisher

[28] Lindgren and Taran 2011 "Business models and Business model innovation in a "Secure and Distributed Cloud Clustering" (DISC) Society". Springer Publishing

[29] Kotter J. 2010 Change Management Macraw Hill

[30] Magretta, J. (2002) Why business models matter?, Harvard Business Review, Vol. 80, No. 5, pp. 86-92.

[31] Markides, C.C. (2008) Game-changing strategies – How to create new market space in established industries by breaking the rules, San Francisco: Jossey-Bass Wiley.

[32] Morris, M.M. Schmindehutte and J. Allen (2003), The entrepreneur's business model: toward a unified perspective, Journal of Business Research, 58(6), pp. 726-735.

[33] Nasa 2011 - Stanford University Workshop 2011 Presentation from Nasa May 2011

[34] Normann & Verganti 2012, Incremental and Radical Innovation incremental and radical innovation: design research versus technology and meaning change Nielsen Norman Group and Politecnico di Milano and Mälardalen University

[35] Osterwalder, A., Pigneur, Y. and Tucci, L.C. (2004) Clarifying business models: Origins, present, and future of the concept, Communications of AIS, No. 16, pp. 1-25.

[36] Osterwalder, A. and Y. Pigneur (2004), An Ontology for E-Business Models, University of Lausanne, Switzerland.

[37] Porter, M. (1980) Competitive strategy: Techniques for analyzing industries and competitors, New York: Free Press.

[38] Porter, M.E. (2011), "The Big Idea: Creating Shared Value - Harvard Business Review - hbr.org › January–February 2011 Shared Value

[39] Porter. M and Michael Kramer (2011) Creating Shared – How to reinvent capitalism – and unlease a wave of Innovation and Growth Harvard Business Review

[40] Prahalad, CK and Hamel, G 'The core competence of the coporation', Harv. Bus. Rev., May-June: 79-91, 1990

[41] Princeton Workshop on Emerging BMs and BMI in Healthcare, Manufacturing and Gaming industry 7 – 8 june 2012 http://riverpublishers.com/river_publisher/series.php?msg=Multi Business Model Innovation and Technologies

[42] Rogers, E. M. (1983) Diffusion of innovations, New York: The Free Press.

[43] Rooke, D Harvard Business review 2005.

[44] Roos, Göran 2009 Key Note speak - IFKAD 2009 conference Glasgow

[45] Rothwell (1994)

[46] Solaimani, Sam 2012 Presentation at the E-challenges Conference 2012 on Business Models – Tooling and Research Agenda Lisabon 2012. http://www.fines-cluster.eu/fines/jm/

[47] Scharmer, C.O. (2009) , Theory U: Leading from the future as it emerges. The social technology of presencing, Berret Koehler, San Francisco

[48] Skarzynski P. and Gibson R. (2008) Innovation to the core, Boston, Harvard Business School Publishing.

[49] Stanford University Workshop with MediaX and Minolta 2010

[50] Stanford University Workshop on Emerging BMs and BMI 18 – 20 may 2011 http://riverpublishers.com/river_publisher/series.php?msg=Multi Business Model Innovation and Technologies

[51] Tidd, J., Bessant, J. and Pavitt, K. (2005) Managing innovation: Integrating technological, market and organizational change, Chichester: John Wiley & Sons.

[52] Tidd, J. and Bessant, J. (2009) Managing innovation: Integrating technological, market and organizational change, Chichester: John Wiley & Sons.

[53] Ulrich, KT & Eppinger, SD 2000, 'Product Design and Development", 2nd edition, Irwin McGraw-Hill.

[54] Vervest, P et al., 2005, Smart Business Networks Springer ISBN 3-540-22840-3

[55] Wallstreet Journal March 2011

[56] Zook, C (2007) Finding Your next core Business Harvard Business review

[57] Zott, Christoph & Amitt & Massa 2011, 'The Business Model: Recent Developments and Future Research' http://ssrn/abstract.com/=1674384

[58] Wall Street Journal Marts 2011

[59] Wall Street Journal April 2011

[60] Wall Street Journal May 2011

[61] WSIE 2012, Boston US - The World Summit on Innovation and Entrepreneurship

[62] www.theWSIE.org. September 26-28, 2012. Boston, US

Biographies

Peter Lindgren is Associate Professor of Innovation and New Business Development at the Center for Industrial Production, Aalborg University, Denmark. He holds B.Sc in Business Administration, M.Sc in Foreign Trade and a Ph.D in Network-based High

Speed Innovation. He has (co-)authored numerous articles and several books on subjects such as product development in network, electronic product development, new global business development, innovation management and leadership, and high speed innovation. His current research interest is in new global business models, i.e. the typology and generic types of business models and how to innovate them.

Rasmus Jørgensen, Post-graduate at Danfoss Automatic Controls Supply Chain department. Automatic Controls is responsible for the global development of controls for refrigeration and air conditioning applications, and Supply Chain ensures the deliveries. In ICI, he is involved in providing and constructing a theoretical background for a business model framework, consisting of seven building blocks. Furthermore, he has been working on ways to digitalize the business model. The framework is currently being prototyped in a brand new 3D-based business model platform together with the company Katalabs. Rasmus has been stationed at ICI's virtual office at Innovation Center Denmark on 200 Page Mill Road, Palo Alto, CA. He is affiliated to the EU-project NEFFICS (Networked Enterprise transFormation and resource management in Future internet enabled Internet CloudS), where he is analyzing the relations between different generations of innovation models and the ICI business model framework.

Conceptualizing strategic business model innovation leadership for business survival and business model innovation excellence

Peter Lindgren[1]

Maizura Ailin Abdullah[2,]

[1]*Department of Mechanical and Manufacturing Engineering, Aalborg University*

[2]*The Royal Institute of Technology (KTH) in Stockholm, Sweden.*

Received 12 February 2013; Accepted: 25 February 2013

Abstract

Too many businesses are being marginalized by blind "business model innovations (BMIs)" and simple "BMIs". As documented in previous research (Markides 2008, Lindgren 2012), most businesses perform BMIs at a reactive level i.e. perceiving what the market, customers and network partners might want rather than what they actually demand.

Few businesses have the ability to proactively lead BMIs and on a strategic level lead BMIs to something that fits the business's long term perspective (Hamel 2011). Apple, Ryanair, Facebook, Zappo are some businesses that have shown BMI Leadership (BMIL) in a proactive way — and more importantly, as some examples of first level BMIL.

The overall aim of the BMIL is to prevent businesses from being marginalized by the BMI and thereby to optimize the business's total BMI investment.

The literature research and case research we studied gave us some important inspiration, themes and baseline for conceptualizing BMIL and to formulate a framework proposing the BMIL strategy process. It also points to some of the requirements that should be taken into consideration and included to become successful via the BMI.

The paper focuses on the following research question:

- "How can businesses gain strategic advantage and learn business survival via BMIL?"

Keywords: Business model innovation, Business Model Innovation Leadership and management

1. Introduction - Why business model innovate?

Miller (1992) questions the notion of being "caught in the middle" or "caught in the innovation spiral". He can be claimed to say that there is a viable middle ground between business innovation strategies. Many businesses have entered a market with success as a niche player or a business focusing on other business model values or different business model values and cost structures (Ryanair, Zara Inditex, Starbuck, Yellow Tail) than established businesses in the industry and gradually expanded their businesses from there to become the leader of their business ecosystem and the BMI process in the business model ecosystem. In some cases, they have even disrupted the existing industry via BMIs. An up-to-date critique of generic innovation and BMI strategies and their limitations, including Porter, appears in Bowman, C. (2008) Generic strategies: a substitute for thinking?

The importance of innovation can however be traced back to the 1930's when Schumpeter first introduced the groundbreaking phenomena of disruptive innovation (Schumpeter 1934). Today, innovation is regarded as a fundamental condition for the survival of societies and businesses, whether they are big or small, even more so if they are small. Businesses are faced with the realities of perpetually-shortening business model life cycles and can no longer depend on short-term tactics, such as lowering costs and implementing minor differentiation or incremental improvements to their multitude of business models. Successful BMIs allow businesses to stay ahead of the competition in terms of cost, performance and development time to market. All these unseen advantages can translate to value to the business, customers and other stakeholders, allowing the business to ultimately stay at the front line of competition —but more importantly, in the frontline of the BMI process.

2. WHY DO BUSINESS NEED TO INNOVATE THEIR BUSINESS MODELS?

One possible answer would be: globalization. Globalization has, in more than one way, dissolved the boundaries between countries, economies, industries and organizations. It has brought about a ripple effect that affects all businesses in many ways. Technologies need to be upgraded, processes must be redesigned, communication has to be faster—all these, just to cope with the ever-changing needs of operations, customers, suppliers and global brands.

One after-effect of globalization is the usage of the Internet and "the cloud" in every day operations. The Internet has freed companies from the traditional ways of doing business, and maintaining relationships and networks. One simple example is BMI in the cloud. The application of "cloud-based BMI" has simply altered the relationships between customers, suppliers, value chains and the BMI processes. Information and knowledge travel faster, beyond measurable paradigms in the cloud. Customers and suppliers are now better-informed and well-educated about potential business models. This creates a power shift, placing the all stakeholders at an advantage in both a "TO BE" and a "AS IS BM" (Lindgren 2012).

The chain reaction goes further. Leading businesses understand the need for increased innovations in product innovation processes and the speed required to innovate products (Fine 1998, Lindgren 2003). In order to stay competitive and gain strategic advantages, businesses now have taken innovations one step higher by incorporating the BMIs (be it radical or incremental BMI) into their strategies. It has been proven that businesses that have introduced and implemented innovation strategies are better able to survive the competitive conditions, compared to companies that have not (Cooper, 2005). However, we still lack evidence that BMIs can prove the same.

All these mentioned above, when strategically combined and implemented, have the potential to improve work processes—product innovation timelines can become shorter, production costs can be lowered, while improving product quality significantly. The speed and efficiency with which innovations are diffused throughout an economy is thought to be critical in increasing productivity and economic growth. In addition, innovations are believed to possess the ability to prolong the survivability and competitiveness of businesses. However research have shown that the most innovative business and countries are not always the winners (O´Brian 2007, Ruchonen 2007) . The issue is to place businesses performing BMIs at an advantageous position in markets via BMI. An advantage possition L, compared to competitors and also other stakeholders.

And yet, innovation research initiatives for the past 50 years have only given us a fragmented understanding within the field of product innovation theory, service innovation theory and organizational theory. These research initiatives have provided us with some basic fundamentals of innovation and pointed out the complexity of innovation—put together, an opportunity to begin to study business model innovation leadership. BMIL attempts to place all the fragmented innovation components together and move our understanding of innovation further to a strategic level, i.e. from a management level to a leadership level. Such a topic reveals some new opportunities and challenges to innovation research, to the industry and the society.

BMIL for us is also about a continuous process of an integrated BMIL model which we propose as focusing on different levels of the BMI. For such a task, the management ideals are insufficient as BMIL requires vision, goals, strategy, sustained belief in BMI's success and a strong commitment to the BMI initiatives. It is about being able to form an integrated overview of the business innovation activities and concurrently "lead" the BMI in a strategic manner, in an ever changing world where a business has continuously to rethink its BMI conditions. It is not just about handling and managing an innovative product development project, rather it is about leading the business "BMI portfolio" strategically, which we shall now elaborate.

This article intends to introduce a brief overview of the available literature on innovation and leadership. Following this, it examines and defines the framework of the BMIL, consequently leading to our framework of the BMIL and thereby leading the BMI portfolio to a strategic advantageous position in the business.

3. THE NATURE OF BMI

BMI can briefly be described as something new, be it a value proposition, customer, value chain, competence, network, relation or a value formula (Lindgren 2012), that changes the basis of the business model —the way the business model is formulated and/or designed. The BMI can be something that is significantly improved, or "based on the results of new developments or new combinations of existing business model blocks.

BMI comes in many different varieties—change of one or more business model block(s), development of a new business model block, change of a business model's relations to other business models either internal or external the business and creation of a new business model ecosystem. BMI is regarded as something so uncertain that the best a business can do is to pour sufficient resources into it and then hope for the best. And, when the businesses are small- and medium-sized enterprises, they are even more dependent on successful outcomes of BMI as compared to large companies.

BMI can be classified into radical and incremental business model innovations (though the terms discontinuous vs. continuous innovation are also used interchangeably) (Balachandra 2000, Leifer 2002, Tidd 2003, Taran 2010). Radical business model innovation occurs very rarely, but the benefit and rewards are exceptionally high, whether they are financial or value-based rewards to the business or beneficial returns the society. Such rare occurrences involve a breakthrough in complexity, radicality and reach (Taran 2010). Radical BMI usually results in a large change in an existing "business model's core" or a new business model. Of course, the degree of radicality is scalable to the time of the BMI process potential measured related to three dimensions as shown in the model in Figure 1.

Incremental BMI, on the other hand, usually involves improvements and small changes in steps which are more progressive in nature. It occurs more frequently and is usually much easier for the business to carry out, simply because it is not as "foreign" and new as something which is a result of the radical BMI. The rule of thumb is that, the more common the business model innovation, the higher the potential of it to be successful. This is because it is more frequently based on tried and tested business models and BMI processes.

BMIs are a major challenge to many businesses today, as they suffer high failure rates within business models. This is due to many different reasons, among them being:

- a predominance of incremental business model innovation, which does not give long-lasting competitive advantages to the business;
- a high failure rate for BMI initiatives. Generally, only few ideas to business models usually reach their market potential, and are only successfully in the early stages of the BMI phase;
- a shorter business model life cycle for new business models, which means that up to 60 to 70% of new business models have to be re-developed within a short time after their introduction;
- limited resources available for BMI (in SMEs) and inefficient BMI resource management in large businesses.

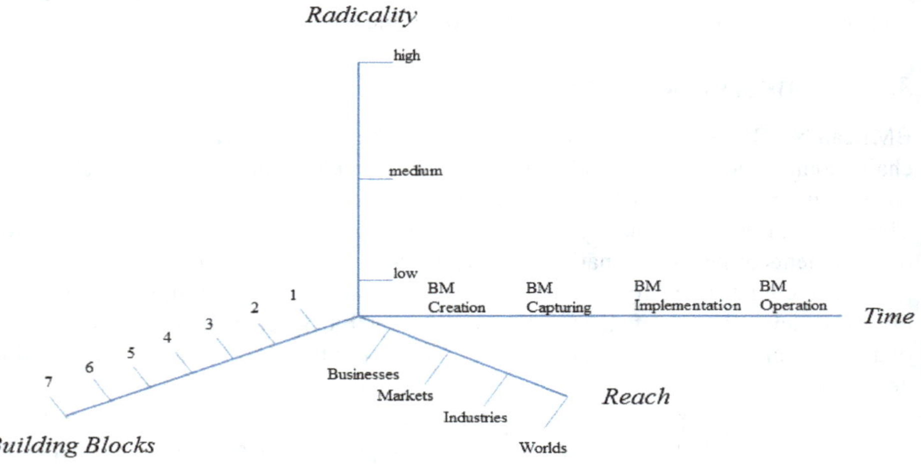

Figure 1. A three dimensional scale of BMI related to the BMI process.

Perhaps, one of the biggest challenges in BMI research is measuring its outcome, efficiency and productivity, as will become evident in the upcoming section. It should be noted, however, that both radical and incremental BMIs are important to the survival of business, as both play important roles in the BMI strategy of business. We claim that the BMI success is not accidental; rather, it is a result of a combination of complex strategy thinking, capturing, dealings and actions, which when combined together, creates the basis of business sustainability. Some of these components of success will be elaborated in the next sections.

4. Research Question

We studied the following research questions:

- How can businesses gain strategic advantages and business survival techniques through the BMIL?

In this context, the paper tries to conceptualize the fundamentals and basis of the BMIL. Second, the paper proposes a BMIL strategy process.

5. Design/Methodology/Approach

The approach is a literature and qualitative research based on research carried out in the timeframe from 2002 to 2012, covering several national and international BMI projects (PUIN project, Newgibm project, ICI project, WIB project and Neffics EU-project funded by the European Commission).

6. Effective and Efficient BMI

As mentioned previously, measuring the outcome and productivity of the BMI is a major challenge in this field. This is because each business around the world has its unique sets of criteria, goals and objectives with relation to its respective business agenda. These businesses then have different resources and varying levels of BMI skills and competences, not excluding knowledge repositories, which influence how business innovation is tackled and achieved in the respective business.

America has always had a history of rewarding creativity and churning out BMIs. However, these trends have been fast fading, according to several research projects (O'Brien 2005, Boston Consulting group 2012, INSEAD 2012, NAM 2012, The World Intellectual Property Organization, Cornell University 2013). As corporate and public nurturing of inventors and scientific research is diminishing in general, there is a need to rethink strategic BMIs not only in the US but also among other western countries. The United States and the EU have been faltering lately and the BMI's efficiency and effectiveness would pay a serious economic and intellectual penalty.

This downward trend is also observed by many institutions e.g. OECD, the National Academy of Sciences, European Commision (Horison 2020 and FP 7), that are very concerned that America and EU will lose their lead in BMIs, and worse still, will not be able to regain their lead. Both American and European politicians are expressing growing concerns on future economic competitiveness of western businesses. Both American and

European business are proposing and even trying out the traditional cures for this downward trend, i.e. cost cutting, educational programs, creating a research and innovation culture, increase in federal funds for research and tax incentives, among others, in order to ensure their lead among the most business model innovative in the world.

During the late 2000's, Europe began to show great interest in BMIs. As a response to this community-wide interest, a succession of initiatives has been introduced to encourage and nurture the BMIs throughout Europe. In March 2012, the European Council launched the "Horizon 2020" which placed BMIs and SMEs in the centre of major policy efforts. Among its many commitments was to make Europe "the most innovative and dynamic knowledge-based economy in the world" by 2010. Such an ambitious effort required a rapid upgrade of EU's business model innovative capacity and an increase in the EU's BMI expenditure. This effort was in response to a report in 2010 which revealed that the EU and America lagged behind Asia in BMI investments.

The fourth Community Innovation Survey (CIS 2008) which prepared the "Innovation policy: updating the Union's approach in the context of the Lisbon strategy" is currently in the field, and CIS 2010 is still being planned and will be underway soon. In 2003, CIS stressed that the "innovation performance in the EU remained below levels recorded in the United States or Japan, and that a lack of innovation activity could be one of the key factors in explaining EU's underperformance in terms of productivity growth in recent years" (Luxembourg: Office for Official Publications of the European Communities 2004, 13).

The Asian region, with two-thirds of the world population, was advancing fast to challenge America's lead in research and innovation in the early 2000´s (Silverthorne 2005) and continue to challenge America. Thus, globally, Asia can be considered one of the largest and fastest-growing investment locations for BMIs. This development continues to offer bigger and bigger potentials where advanced BMIs are concerned, and America and Europe cannot afford to ignore this direction of BMI growth that is occurring in Asia but also in Latin America and Africa.

It is no question that the Asian region is gearing up and looking forward to the next wave of BMIs (in the form of combined disciplines of BMIL). Japan, China and India are investing heavily within the new technologies of the BMI. With the rising usage of the cloud in business model practices, it is not difficult for businesses to create, capture, deliver and consume network-based business models across businesses, markets, industries and worlds.

But, is increased investment allocation and spending in the BMIs and creative BMI labs really the solution, or rather the ONLY solution, to success? Businesses, be them "large" or SMEs, in their bid to reach the finishing line of a successful BMI, might actually bypass the golden edge of BMI success without even realizing it.

Businesses have definitely benefited from the Internet's and cloud's ability to "send" work easily around the globe. But, this is not to say that this is without problems. Businesses face fragmentation in their BMI strategy and policies, which are usually in conflict with other business models internal to the business but also with customers, network partners and other stakeholders' BMI strategies and policies. Bureaucracy is difficult to penetrate, leading to imprecise fund allocation to the right BMI projects. More importantly, businesses, in general, are lacking the BMI culture that encourages creative and strategic BMI. The gap between industry and academia is too large, hindering free exchange of ideas and flow of information about BMIL, while education and research institutes do nothing to encourage an innovation culture of experimentation and hardly focus on how do we bring the business model ideas to the market and make them grow and benefit the businesses. The gap between academia and practitioners often lies in their differences of interests and values related to the BMI. The academia focuses upon improving and increasing innovations without thinking about the cost, efficiency and long-term benefits of the investment. The practitioners focus on their businesses and bottomline without opening up and releasing their real potentials in their business and business models. All these factors place tremendous pressure on society's management and investment in business development to create, capture, deliver and consume the successes of BMI initiatives and investment to gain long-term efficiency, effectiveness and learning. A new BMI agenda is needed both by academia, practitioners and society. An agenda that would be initially created as a network-based and would open the BMI platform in the clouds.

7. THE NATURE OF BMIL

BMIL is also a major challenge to businesses today. So far, studies on leadership related to the BMI have mainly attempted to provide guidance on how to define the leader's task and role from a management perspective while focusing on leadership competences and characteristics (Bryman 2004; Rooke 2005). These studies mainly concern discussions on individual leadership, as well as collective leadership (leadership by several managers in a group or as a team internal a business), but not leadership across different businesses and business models (both internal and external). In this context, "leadership in the clouds" is a concept where business managers have to carry out BMIL in the clouds together with other managers from different businesses. There are many studies on organizational leadership inside businesses, where the leadership of a business and various characteristics of leadership seen from a managerial, strategical and tactical perspective. When debating BMI, such studies mostly covered the management of single BMI projects, however, most often at a tactical level. In all these, leadership studies rarely focused on the strategic leadership of the BMI and further these studies do not take into consideration that the world and the BMI game has changed over the last 10–15 years taking the field of BMI to the clouds, to a network-based and open BMI-based context.

Dennis *et al.* emphasized years ago how the strategic BMIL phenomenon should look like, by presenting four main areas:

1. Strategic leadership as a **collective phenomenon**—where the strategic leadership of business models and BMIs requires contribution from more than a single individual business or business model.
2. Strategic leadership of BMI is a **processual phenomenon**—leaders need to mobilize other stakeholders in a system of interrelationships, rather than what they are.
3. Strategic leadership of BMI as a **dynamic phenomenon**—consists of the emergence, development, conduct, impact, performance and learning of management teams. This research area deals with the dynamic construction, deconstruction and reconstruction of BMIL roles over time according to the present context of the business, portfolio of business models, business model and its building blocks together with the business model ecosystems that the business is operating in.

4. Strategic leadership of BMI as a **supra-organisational phenomenon**—BMIL roles and influences on such roles extend beyond focal business and business model boundaries. Here, collective BMIL must mobilize support and lead relationships, not only within the business, but also within its network to optimize the business performance of BMIs.

Porter (1985), Kotler (1994) and Malhotra (2000) have taken quite a different approach to BMIL, which they term **market leadership**. Malhotra defines market leadership as a business leading its position in a particular market or line of business and sees this as an optimum type of leadership. Kotler stresses the importance of having a defending market leadership. And, Porter proposes how to achieve market leadership, i.e. via cost leadership, differentiation or a focus strategy. However, none of these authors have mentioned achieving leadership via BMI i.e. BMIL.

Studies in the area of BMI have, quite surprisingly, hardly touched upon leading the market via strategic BMIs. Businesses that wish to ensure continued growth or competitiveness need to select one or more BMI champion(s), i.e. the right BMI leader who will have the BMIL skills, charisma and determination to lead the business portfolio of the BMI initiative. Taking into consideration the various theories discussed, we can ask the question "Is there a specific and distinctive form of BMIL?" And, considering the many different components of BMIs mentioned above, Is a different BMIL profile needed for today's BMI game? Our answer to this is a clear – Yes!

The significance of BMIs is widely acknowledged in a range of organizations, societies and in global competition. Thus, it is important for businesses to develop the ability to lead BMIs and to understand what BMIL is all about. The BMI is an ongoing, never-ending strategic process. Though there are available literature on managing innovation, they address mostly and mainly the issue of business survival. BMIL, however, has many more aspects to it than just management. Today, businesses have to lead themselves into the very core of the BMI process and make their businesses stay here via BMIs. Otherwise, they will suffer the role of being marginalized in the BMI process which, as we see, several western businesses both large and small business are doing today. That is one major reason to why western countries are losing businesses and jobs because they are not creating new and sustainable businesses.

8. THE FRAMEWORK OF BMIL

Many researchers have attempted to provide their notions on what aspects to consider when discussing innovation. For instance, how to define the product innovation development task (Roseneau 1983; Leifers 2002), how to characterize the field of product innovation development (Sanchez 1996: Child & Faulkner 1998; Goldman & Price 1998; Bohn & Lindgren 2003; Price 2005, (Bessant 1999), how to define the success criteria of product innovation development (Balachandra 1983; Boer 2002; Bohn & Lindgren 2004), the characteristics of the product innovation development model (Cooper 1986; Corso 2002; Cooper 2004; Bessant 1999; Christensen 2003), and identifying and choosing the right enablers for high-speed product innovation development (Fine 1998, Lindgren 2003).

Few have, in addition, tried to answer the questions of Why is leadership in BMI important to business companies? and, How are BMILs implemented in businesses? Cooper (2005) has commenced research in the area by focusing on product leadership as a pathway to profitable BMI, presenting four points of performance of his Innovation

Diamond: strategy of the business company, portfolio of BMI activities, process for new product development and the climate of the business company (how successful senior managers are in creating and fostering an business innovative culture). However, Cooper in his work only touches upon fragments of the complete pallet of BMIL opportunities.

Until now, studies have predominantly focused on the business's individual management of BMIs, particularly, as in Coopers case, the product innovation development which is just part of the value proposition building block and part of the BMI and the BMI process that starts from an idea and concept and ends when the business company prototype is ready to launch the business model to product in the market. Our notion of BMIL should not, however, be confused nor used interchangeably with the current ideas of BMI management of market leadership. It is an ideology on how to lead the different components and the business's BMI portfolio via the innovation leadership in a framework called BMIL, in order to achieve more strategic BMI success. Our definition of BMI success is strongly related to the leadership of "the core of the BMI process" via BMI which is strongly related to the long-term vision, mission, goals and strategies.

According to our research understanding, the management of business model product innovation today takes place mostly at an individual and tactical mid-management level. As a starting point and for a summary on how we visualize the difference between business model innovation management (BMIMA) and business model innovation leadership (BMIL), please refer to Table 1.

In the BMI context, we differentiate between BMIL and BMIMA. We consider BMIL as related to the strategic part of BMI and BMIMA as related to the tactical level of BMI (Lindgren 2003).

BMIL focusses on:
How to strategically and proactively lead the business portfolio of BMs and BMI activities into the core of the BMI process?

BMIMA focusses on:
How to tactically and proactively manage the business portfolio of BMs and BMI activities in the core of the BMI process?

BMIL´s overall aim is to bring the business into a better strategic BMI position and thereby into the core of the BMI process where the business has the opportunity to actively lead the game of BMI. The opposite position would leave the business with no opportunities to influence and change the BMI processes irrespective of whether the enterprise wants to join and change the BMI processes. This is not a preferable strategic position.

Up to this point, we claim that discussion and research on BMIs leave us with a rather fragmented picture of BMIL. In our mind, only one-seventh of the total BMIL has the potential. There seems to be hardly any research with specific focus on the combination of BMIL, the BMI portfolio and what is more, the strategic role that BMIL can play in businesses. The research until today on this topic is mainly related to organizational leadership dimension of BMIL, which is of course necessary, but quiet different to what we define as the BMIL.

Table 1 A basic summary of the differences between innovation management and innovation leadership.

Business Model Innovation Management (BMIMA)	Business Model Innovation Leadership (BMIL)
Short-term objectives relying on tactics	Long-term objectives built upon strategy and strategical objectives.
Internal focus with importance placed at the operational and implementation levels.	Internal focus stressing on operational and implementation levels PLUS external focus at the strategic level and integration with tactical level.
Success criteria based on cost, time, (superior) performance of BMI.	Success criteria based on continuous improvement and continuous innovation, learning, and innovation knowledge and capability development.
Prefers only minor performance improvements that can be provided by incremental BMIs.	Supports incremental innovation, but focus, at the same time, advocates riskier, radical innovation and BMI.
Depends mostly on organizational competences.	Depends on innovating organizational competences, and at the same time, encourages the exploration and exploitation of external sources of BMI competences, i.e. network partners' BMI competence.
Most of the time concentrates on one BMI project and process at a time.	Leads a portfolio of business model innovative projects and processes consisting of a balance of both incremental and radical BMI leadership process.
Stresses high speed BMI.	Stresses right speed for the BMI.
The business has an internal, almost short-sighted view of the BMI process as it does not follow through with the BMI process once the business model "leaves" the BMI phase and enters the business, market, industry and worlds. A transaction business model innovation approach. Elements of stakeholder feedback on BMI proposals are often regarded as after-BMI services.	The business has an overall view of the BMIL process and is located at the center of the BMIL process. This way, the business can strategically position itself in the market by exploiting and implementing the BMI.

A holistic, strategic concept of the BMIL is, therefore, still lacking. We find this rather peculiar, considering the importance that is being placed on the BMI and its strategy.

In this article, innovation leadership is more than product development or product leadership. A good starting point in defining our BMIL strategy process, therefore, should commence with identifying the strategic task of BMI, defining the context of BMI and defining the success criteria of BMI.

Table 2 Short-term and long-term success criteria for BMIL.

Short-term success criteria	Long-term success criteria
Time Cost (perceived and actual) Value (perceived and actual) Performance	Time, i.e. right speed, right cost, right performance Continuous improvement Continuous BMI Learning BMI efficiency BMI effectiveness Placed in the core of the BMI process Leading the BMI process

The model of BMIL strategy process is shown in Figure 2. The figure starts with the analyzing and choosing process among the different types of strategic types of BMIs that businesses can and should follow in order to accomplish both short-term and long-term success of business model innovation, finally ending up with BMI strategy implementation, control, adjustment and correction.

Our proposed framework for business model innovation leadership introduces eight main focus areas to consider.

1. The building block dimension.
2. The business model dimension.

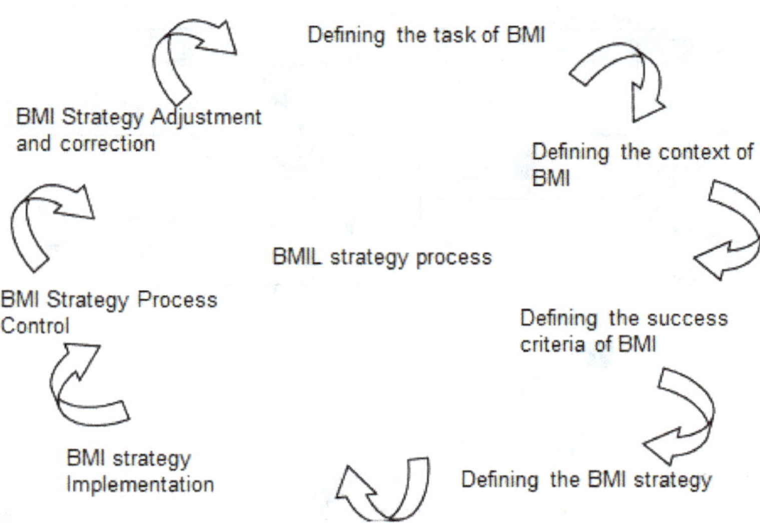

Figure 2 The BMIL strategy process.

3. The BMI dimension related to the creative part (both on AS IS and TO BE BMs) of BMI.
4. The BMI dimension related to the capturing, delivering and consuming part which we call "act and do" part of BMI.
5. The BMIL dimension—different viewpoints of BMI.
6. The portfolio dimension of a business, in this case, the integration and synergy between different business models and BMI projects on different models in the business.
7. The BMIL Strategy dimension—a business BMI strategy related to different phases in a BMI process.
8. The BMI strategy related to different business model ecosystems.

These eight BMIL areas have to be led individually, as well as together.

9. Findings and Discussion

Perhaps, one way of visualizing the effectiveness and efficiency of a BMIL is to implement it in a innovation leadership portfolio and canvas.

Many CEOs we studied believed in pouring a large part of their resources into just one area of BMIL i.e. value proposition innovation leadership with high-investment, high-risk projects, with a belief that this one project is their only "golden egg" which will provide them with a jackpot of returns. Achieving success this way can often be attributed to pure luck. Such projects usually involve radical innovation and new knowledge. What happens is that the project would require sophisticated knowledge and thinking and it supersedes the project innovation timeframe. When this happens, the project usually requires further injection of investment, year after year, draining the available innovation resources from the business. Eventually, the BMI project is deemed unfruitful and the management is forced to pull the plug on the project, at the expense of many years of

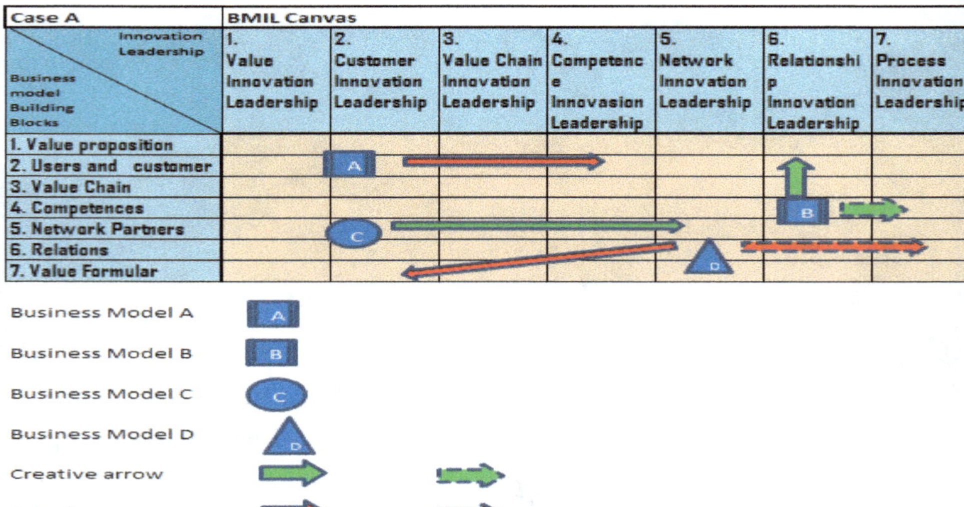

Figure 3 "TO BE" BM and "AS IS" BM in the BMIL Canvas – a case.

research and development and business resources that could have been deployed to other BMI areas and projects.

Just as investments can be made in portfolio style, so can a business's investment for business innovation projects—which in this case, we shall label as a "BMI portfolio". The idea is to diversify a business's resources, selecting a mix of business innovation projects to invest in and run, thus spreading the business innovation investment risk among different types of business innovation projects, according to the following factors.

It is believed that in the field of finance, portfolio analysis considers investors to be risk averse meaning that given two assets that offer the same expected return, investors will prefer the less risky one. Likewise, in an innovation portfolio, we assume that managers usually prefer to invest in innovation projects which are less riskier and require fewer resources. And, though they have a higher success rate, they provide lower returns, which do not contribute much to a business's profit margin (Leifers 2002).

A business's innovation portfolio in this sense should ideally consist of several carefully and strategical elected BMI projects of varying degrees of BMI initiatives. These projects should, at the same time, reflect the varying amounts of investments (whether financial, manpower or physical) needed to drive the respective BMI projects. The amount of investment assigned to each BMI portfolio item should depend on several factors, among them being:

- The type of BMI project being developed—whether it is a known BMI project that is available to the customers or a completely new business model that has not been seen before by market, industry or the world.
- The type of BMI that shall be utilized—whether incremental or radical innovation. We should also mention that this factor is closely related to the earlier factor of whether it is a known or new business model.
- The perceived receptivity of the business model in the market—customer and network partners' perceptions can help in the cases of known business models using incremental innovation. However, in the case of completely new business models being developed using radical business model innovation, there are available opinions that agree that e.g. just market research cannot satisfy this one factor (Christensen 1997, Drucker 1985, Cooper 2005).
- The expected timeline of the BMI project has the disadvantage of high development costs, long-term development periods and uncertain success rates.

The final factor that should be considered, just as in any BMI portfolio, is the risk factor. The risk assigned to each BMI portfolio component, whether it is a network-based BMI project, a BMI process project or a high-risk BMI project (with a high probability of failing, which also means that it probably requires more investment, which means that if it is successful it will result in higher returns, and if it fails, it will conversely result in higher losses) or a low-risk project (with a high probably of success, but demands low investment, and does not result in high returns when it is successful).

Having these factors in mind for a BMI portfolio will make a drawing of the strategic BMI leadership map of the business innovation leadership model more effective, in other words, which component deserves more attention and resources, at which stage of e.g.

BMI phase and "the business model lifecycle" should we pay more attention and investment.

Finding the perfect balance and combination of our proposed BMIL components is our interpretation of how to begin to lead BMI more strategically and bring business into BMIL.

10. CONCLUSION

BMI is not a new concept in business. However, the idea of continuous and sustainable BMI is fairly new. Businesses must learn to identify the opportunities of BMIL, react faster to changes in the field of BMIL and produce new BMI roads of BMIL faster, while balancing value, time, and cost together with continues innovation, continues improvement and learning. It is partly because of such dramatic changes in the game of the BMIs that BMIL has become a crucial and necessary ingredient for business growth and survival.

This, thus, triggers an urgent need for a new and improved thinking about leadership of BMIs. This is because business survival depends on the ability of its leaders to develop creative responses to the different types of challenges facing the BMI portfolio and BMIL. For successful implementation, top management must undertake a holistic approach to implementation and align the business innovations strategically, effectively and efficiently, both from a short-term and especially a long-term perspective.

BMIL is about developing and implementing a superior capability to innovate business models. It forces both an "outside" and an inside" look at the BMIL processes. This "outside look" manifests itself in the ability to integrate the BMI entities and processes external to the business (hence, outsiders) and integrating them into the business, making them part of the business innovation leadership strategy. The "inside look" manifests itself in the ability to integrate the BMI entities and processes internal to the business (hence, insiders) and integrating them into the different BMI projects and processes, making them part of the business innovation leadership culture. Fulfilling this BMIL vision, related goals and strategy brings the businesses into a position of leading the BMI process—a proactive BMIL strategy opposite to a reactive BMIL strategy, thereby into a strategy advantage position via strategic BMI.

This article introduced a slightly different approach to using the BMI in order to enable a business to achieve superior strategic reach and BMI position. Focusing on factors internal to the business (such as the business model blocks, business models, business model portfolio innovation process of the business), as well as external factors such as the business model ecosystem innovation process and hereunder the network-based BMI process. The aim of this process of BMI implementing the BMIL in the business is to place the business in a more central and strategic BMI position i.e.in the core of the BMI process. This allows the business to have an overall view of the BMI process, influence the BMI process and react earlier to forthcoming BMI processes. In this way, the business can strategically position itself as the leader of the market and become the leader of the BMI process by exploiting and implementing innovation.

Our proposal to the concept of BMIL is, therefore, different to what has already been said. The differences are mainly related to a move from tactical management of BMI to a more strategic BMI focusing on the strategical advantage in the business model ecosystems via BMIL.

Further, our concept of BMIL is more holistic involving seven dimensions of strategic BMIs i.e. value innovation leadership, customer innovation leadership, value chain innovation leadership, competence innovation leadership, network innovation leadership, relations innovation leadership and process innovation leadership. This forms the BMIL "umbrella" and potential that has to be orchestrated.

11. FUTURE EXPECTED RESULTS/CONTRIBUTION

We expect, in future research, to find more tools and methods for the BMIL. We expect that these will influence the possibilities for implementing BMIL.

12. REFERENCES

[1] Abell, D. F.., "Defining the Business: The Starting Point of Strategic Planning" New Jersey: Prentice-Hall, Inc., 1980.

[2] Balachandra, R. and Friar, J. H., "Managing New Product Development Processes the Right Way," 1 (1999) 33-43, Information Knowledge Systems Management, IOS Press

[3] "Factors for Success in R&D Projects and New Product Innovation: A Contextual Framework," (August 1997) IEE Transactions on Engineering Management, Vol. 44, No. 3

[4] Bessant, John. Challenges in Innovation Management. Brighton: Centre for Research in Innovation Management, 1999

[5] Bohn, K & Lindgren, P, 2002, 'Right Speed in Network Based Product Development and the Relationship to Learning, CIM and CI', CINet, Helsinki.

[6] Boer, H and Gertsen F From Continuous Improvement to Continuous Innovation: A (retro)(per)spective, International Journal of Technology Management.

[7] Bryman, A. "Qualitative research on Leadership: A critical but appreciative review." The Leadership Quarterly, 2004.

[8] Bowman, C. (2008)

[9] The Global Innovation Index by The Boston Consulting Group 2012 is a global index developed as a one off exercise back in 2009. It measures the level of innovation of a country. It is produced jointly by The Boston Consulting Group (BCG), the National Association of Manufacturers (NAM), and The Manufacturing Institute (MI), the NAM's nonpartisan research affiliate. NAM described it as the "largest and most comprehensive global index of its kind".

[10] The Global Innovation Index by INSEAD,

[11] The World Intellectual Property Organization 2013

[12] Child, J & Faulkner D,1998, 'Strategies of Co-operation – Managing Alliances, Networks, and Joint Ventures', Oxford University Press, Oxford.

[13] Casadesus-Masanell Ramon and Joan Enric Ricart From Strategy to Business Models and onto Tactics Long Range Planning 43 (2010) 195e215

[14] Cornell University 2012

[15] Chesbrough, H. (2003). The Era of Open Innovation. MIT Sloan Management Review, 44 (3), 1-9.

[16] Chesbrough, Henry (2006), Open Business Models:How to Thrive in the New Innovation Landscape, Boston: Harvard Business School Press.

[17] Chesborough, H. (2007) Open business models. How to thrive in the new innovation landscape, Boston: Harvard Business School.

[18] Chesbrough 2011 Keynote Speech at the Oslo innovation week October 2011

[19] Christensen Clayton and M. Johnson, What are Business Models, and How are they Built? Harvard Business School Note 9-610-019(2009)

[20] Christensen, Clayton M. The innovator's dilemma: when news technology cause great firms to fail. Boston: Harvard Business School Press, 1997.

[21] Cooper, Robert G. Product Leadership: Pathways to Profitable Innovation, 2nd ed. New York: Basic Books, 2005.

[22] Cooper, R, 1993 'Winning at New Products' Addison-Wesley Publishing Company ISBN 0-201-56381-91993

[23] Fine, C.H. Clockspeed, Perseus Book, 1998

[24] Francis, D. and Bessant, J. (March 2005). Technovation. "Targeting innovation and implications for capability development" Volume 25, Issue 3, March 2007, pp. 171-183

[25] Goldman, Nagel & Price, 1998, 'Agile Competitors and Virtual Organisations', Van Nostrand Reinhold, New York.

[26] Hayward, Bob M. "Innovation in Asia/Pacific and Japan Becoming World-Class." Gartner, March 10, 2006. Downloaded from http://www.gartner.com/DisplayDocument?id=489655&ref=g_sitelink on 25th December 2007.

[27] Horizon 2020 and FP 7 European Commision http://ec.europa.eu/research/fp7/index_en.cfm

[28] Johnson M.W., Christensen, M.C. and Kagermann, H. (2008) Reinventing your business model, Harvard Business Review, vol. 86 No. 12, pp. 50-59

[29] Johnson M., C. Christensen and H. Kagermann, Reinventing your business model, Harvard Business Review 86(12) (2008);

[30] Jia Hepeng. "China needs to encourage 'bottom-up' innovation." Science and Development Network, October 12, 2007.

[31] Kotler, Philip, Marketing Management: Analysis, Planning, Implementation and Control, (town unknown): Prentice-Hall, 1994

[32] Leifer, R. Critical Factors Predicting Radial Innovation Success. New York: Rensselaer Polytechnic Institute, December 2002.

[33] Lindgren, P. "Network Based High Speed Product Innovation" (ISBN 87-91200-15-6) PhD diss, Center for Industrial Production, Aalborg University, 2003.

[34] Lindgren P., 2012 Business Model Innovation Leadership: How Do SME´s Strategically Lead Business Model Innovation? I: International Journal of Business and Management, Vol. 7, Nr. 14, 07.2012, s. 53-75.

[35] Markides C. , Game-Changing Strategies: How to Create New Market Space in Established Industries by Breaking the Rules, Jossey-Bass, San Francisco (2008).

[36] Magretta, J. (2002) Why business models matter? Harvard Business Review, Vol. 80, No. 5, pp. 86-92.

[37] Malhotra 2000 (other details unknown).

[38] Miller (1992)

[39] Neffics 2011/2012 Baseline analysis of Business Values D 3.1., D 3.2. and Business Model innovation leadership D 4.1., D 4.2., D.4.3 the Neffics project 2012 www.neffics.eu

[40] O'Brien, Timothy L. "Are U.S. Innovators Losing Their Competitive Edge?" International Herald Tribune, November 13, 2005, Technology & Media section. Downloaded from http://www.iht.com/articles/2005/11/14/business/invent.php on 25th December, 2007.

[41] Organisation for Economic Co-operation and Development (OECD). "Measuring Innovation in OECD and non-OECD countries." (ISBN 0-7969-2062-1) Human Sciences Research Council, Cape Town, South Africa, 2006.

[42] Osterwalder, A, Y. Pigneur and L.C. Tucci (2004), Clarifying business models: Origins, present, and future of the concept, Communications of AIS, No. 16, pp. 1-25.

[43] Osterwalder et all 2010 Business Model Generation

[44] Padma, T. V. "India 'lagging behind' in innovation race." Science and Development Network, October 15, 2007.

[45] Porter, Michael E., Competitive Advantage. New York: The Free Press, 1985.

[46] Porter, M. E. (2011), Creating Shared Value: Redefining Capitalism and the Role of the Corporation in Society, Harvard Business Review,

[47] Rosenau, M.D., Managing the Development of the New Products, ITP, pp. 39-41., 1993

[48] Rooke, D. Harvard Business Review, 2005 (other details unknown).

[49] Ruchonen Juha (2007) Victa – Virtual ICT Accelerator Technology Review 219/2007 Teces, Finland

[50] Sanchez, R 2000b, 'Product, Process, and Knowledge Architectures in Organizational Competence', Research Working Paper, Oxford University Press, 2000-11.

[51] Sanchez, R 1996a, 'Strategic Product Creation: Managing New Interactions of Technology, Markets and Organizations', European Management Journal Vol 14. No 2, pp 121-138.

[52] Silverthorne, Sean. "The Rise of Innovation in Asia." Harvard Business School, March 7, 2005. Downloaded from http://hbswk.hbs.edu/item/4676.html on 25th December, 2007.

[53] Taran, Yariv Rethinking it All : Overcoming Obstacles to Business Model Innovation. Aalborg : Center for Industrial Production, Aalborg University, 2011. 193 p. Publication: Research › Ph.d. thesis

[54] Tidd, J., Bessant, J. & Pavitt, K., Managing Innovation: Integrating Technological, Market and Organizational Change, 3rd ed. New Jersey: John Wiley & Sons Ltd., 2003.

[55] Ulrich, KT & Eppinger, Product Design and Development. 2nd ed, San Diego: Irwin McGraw-Hill, 2000.

[56] Wind, Yuromoram. "A New Procedure for Concept Evaluation." Journal of Marketing (October 1973): 2-11.

[57] Scozzi 2012 Different Practice to implement Open Innovation Ifkad conference 2012

[58] Shafer S. M., H. J. Smith and J. C. Linder, The Power of Business Models, Business

[59] Horizons 48, 199e207 (2005).

[60] Taran, Y., Boer, H., & Lindgren, P. (2009). Theory Building - Towards an Understanding of Business Model Innovation Processes. Aalborg University, Centre for Industrial Production, Denmark.

[61] Teece David J. (2011) Business Models, Business Strategy and Innovation Long Range Planning 43/2-3 April/May 2010

[62] Ulrich, KT & Eppinger, SD 2000, 'Product Design and Development", 2nd edition, Irwin McGraw-Hill.

[63] X. Lecoq, B. Demil and V. Warnier, Le Business Model, un Outil d'Analyse Strate´gique, L'Expansion Management Review 123, 50e59 (2006).´

[64] Zott, C., and Amitt, R., and Mazza, L. (2010) The Business Model: Theoretical roots, recent developments, and future research. Madrid, Spain: IESE Business Shoolo, Ducument Number)

Biographies

Peter Lindgren is Associate Professor of Innovation and New Business Development at the Center for Industrial Production, Aalborg University, Denmark. He holds B.Sc in Business Administration, M.Sc in Foreign Trade and Ph.D in Network-based High Speed Innovation. He has (co-)authored numerous articles and several books on subjects such as product development in network, electronic product development, new global business development, innovation management and leadership, and high speed innovation. His current research interest is in new global business models, i.e. the typology and generic types of business models and how to innovate them.

Maizura Ailin Abdullah is a PhD researcher at the Royal Institute of Technology (KTH) in Stockholm, Sweden. She is attached to the Integrated Product Development group of the Department of Machine Design, under the School of Industrial Engineering of Management. At KTH, her research areas include Open Innovation, Business Models and Networking within Open Innovation scenarios.

Index

www.ingramcontent.com/pod-product-compliance
Lightning Source LLC
Chambersburg PA
CBHW061607220326
41598CB00024BC/3476

* 9 7 8 8 7 9 3 3 7 9 4 1 1 *